THREE YEARS IN THE KLONDIKE

A GOLD MINER'S LIFE IN DAWSON CITY, 1898-1901

By Jeremiah Lynch

The Narrative Press
P.O. Box 2487, Santa Barbara, California 93120 U.S.A.
Telephone: (805) 884-0160 Web: www.narrativepress.com

ISBN1-58976-096-4 (Paperback)
ISBN 1-58976-097-2 (eBook)

Produced in the United States of America

TABLE OF CONTENTS

Chapter 1

FRISCO TO DAWSON

On June 11, 1898, the new steamship *St. Paul* left San Francisco for St. Michaels with 275 passengers, bound for the Klondike via the mouth of the Yukon River. A faint rumour of the misfortunes that had occurred to many of those who essayed the Chilkoot Pass the previous winter already pervaded the city, and partially induced others, as well as myself, to choose the longer but safer water route.

In a week we came to Dutch Harbour, in the Aleutian Islands, where the *St. Paul* anchored three days to coal. Other steamers and sailing-vessels were there and at Unalaska, three miles distant, all laden with passengers for the Klondike. Three thousand people, including scores of women, were of the number; we made a strangely assorted assemblage with our motley costumes. A shipload from Boston, which had arrived six weeks earlier, was camped on the shore, waiting for the ice to break in the Behring Sea, and also for a steamer that had been chartered to carry them to St. Michaels.

These adventurers were mainly from the New England and Middle States. They were ill-prepared to live in tents, and suffered cruelly in the cold mist, which was never absent. The steamer owners or charterers had contracted to land them at St. Michaels, but had disembarked them at Unalaska instead, and then sent the vessel back to Seattle for additional supplies. No provision had been made for this exigency, and many lacked shelter, clothing, food, and money. It may be thought that people, especially women, should not have ventured on such an expedition without some means. But if we all had wealth there would be no more enterprise, and the world would be stagnant.

Several river steamboats for the Yukon were in process of building at the island. They were constructed to draw but 4 feet of water, fully equipped and loaded, with ample space for 150 passengers and 200 tons freight. When completed they would be towed to St. Michaels, it being deemed hardly safe for such shallow craft to traverse the thousand miles of sea with their own steam.

I wandered in the bleak, muggy atmosphere for the three miles separating Unalaska and Dutch Harbour, and over the soggy ground covered with tents and filled with anxious, worried faces. No sun was visible; it was rain, snow, or mist, or all three combined; not a cheerful halting-point on the way to wealth. The land directly back from the shores was barren, desolate, and mountainous, with neither trees nor shrubbery.

A small Russian church, two or three trading stores, log huts and tents for employes of the ship agencies and for the artisans imported to build the boats – no more. It gave us all the blues; for if this was the land and climate at Unalaska, how much worse must it not be a thousand miles still farther into the frozen North?

I looked over our 3,000, very carefully, for it was my interest to know the manner of people who were to be both my rivals and companions in exploiting the new land of gold. None seemed very rich, few very poor. There were neither capitalists nor paupers. None were very old, none were very young. Perhaps two-thirds were from the United States, largely from the Pacific coast. Of the remaining third a goodly proportion were Swedes. Those who are born in cold climes preferably seek the same in other lands; and the reverse seems to be true. For there were very few Italians, Mexicans, or Spaniards, and a scant number of French; and the same rule I found to hold afterwards during my sojourn in the Klondike, with the exception, of course, of the French-Canadians, the Canayens, who are the voyageurs of all this Northern world of ice and snow.

Of the 3,000, very few were in ill health, and if they were poor in everything else, they were rich in good constitutions and robust frames. Even the women seemed to expect all kinds of physical difficulties up north, and were stoically prepared. But withal I gleaned in conversations that not many of the men had ever lived or laboured in a mining country, and while possessing fortitude were yet very ignorant, both of what had to be done and if they could do it. The sombre weather was typical of their mood. Though many had been here for weeks, I never knew of but one small social entertainment. No music, no dances, no walks or little dinners. All were thinking either of what was before or what had been left behind, and all were fearful, yet anxious, to go ahead, to push on, without delay, to the goal.

They were a picked body of Argonauts, chosen from the entire world, and capable of wresting the gold, and with it a new continent, from the clutches of the frozen North, where both have lain unfound and unexplored since the beginning.

We left Dutch Harbour on June 23, and in two days were slowly steaming amid the ice-floes of the Behring

Sea. From the topmast nothing but ice and water could be seen; yet withal it was so shallow that the boatswain kept constantly dropping the lead.

Forty miles from shore in the Behring Sea, and only 10 feet of water under our prow! This is caused by the Yukon River bringing down in its spring freshets trees, earth, and brush, in vast quantities, that lodge on the shallow eastern shores of the sea. For hundreds of miles along the eastern littoral of the Alaskan coast-line this extraordinary phenomenon exists, and eventually the Arctic Ocean will be an inland sea, and people will walk from North America to Asia dry-shod.

Behring Sea is more a strait than a sea, and no strong current nor strong tides exist to move this immense mass of debris delivered from the mouths of the Yukon River. It therefore lies passive and sluggish, slipping farther and farther into the narrow channel separating Siberia from that part of Alaska adjoining the Yukon. The result is certain, though distant. For the same reason the ocean steamers pass the several navigable mouths of the Yukon at such a distance that these are invisible from the masthead, and continuing further north in the narrow channel round by the north-east, anchor in the harbour of the island of St. Michaels, sixty miles above the mouth of the Yukon river. We made slow progress, slipping by and between ice-floes, on which a stray seal could at times be seen, plunging into the water as we neared his trysting-place.

There was no wind, and apparently less current. The floes were not large, and were constantly breaking in to smaller pieces under the influence of a warmer latitude, for they had come from the Arctic Ocean. The next morning when we came on deck we found ourselves in the Bay of

St. Michaels, and counted twenty-two deep-sea sailing vessels and steamships at anchor. All these had arrived before us, and each one had brought passengers and supplies for the Klondike, which was 1,600 miles distant up the Yukon.

We had our first sample of the Alaskan mosquito, and he sustained his wide reputation. He was voracious and pertinacious. He easily penetrated an ordinary kid glove, and was of abnormal size. He came in uncounted clouds, and the new-comers were his especial favourites. Nothing could prevent his attacks, and we found that the safest place was on the *St. Paul*, anchored half a mile from shore. Few only even of the most bloodthirsty dared that wide stretch of water, to meet a quick and sudden demise.

The island had but one poor hotel, and no town at all; only a few dwelling-houses and warehouses belonging to the trading companies, and tents for a company of United States soldiers, who were camping with the mosquitoes. Innumerable dogs, guarded by a few squalid Indians, gave life and spirit to the place. Of course there were ourselves – 5,000 or 6,000 of us – but nearly all living on our respective vessels, for the steamer companies on the "outside" had sold passenger tickets direct to Dawson, allowing for all detentions. Thus we remained twelve days at St. Michaels on the *St. Paul*, awaiting the arrival of the first river boat down the Yukon from Dawson. It was a dreary detention. The *St. Paul* was for ever unloading her cargo by lighters. It cost a dollar for the return journey to the shore, where there was nothing to see, the whole country being covered with patches of dark moss, to be later described, with which I then first made acquaintance. Fishing was good, and we were plentifully supplied with salmon and smaller fish, all of most excellent quality. Besides, there were our neighbours, both on the *St. Paul* and the other vessels, with whom we gradually became more or less acquainted.

The usual recreation, when a boat could be procured, was rowing from one vessel to another in the quiet waters, and asking continual queries about where they were going and where they came from, and when. Everyone was avid for information from the Klondike, and also from Rampart, Tanana, and other intervening rivers and territories.

The old Russian fort still existed, and had been turned into a mess and dining room by the Alaska Commercial Company. A few of the old cannon were littered about, and remnants of the old Russian wharf could be seen at low-tide. There was not a tree on the island, which was a dozen miles or more in diameter, with very small hills or, rather, elevations. One could not walk into the interior, with its marshes covered by thin ice and the soul-harassing clumps of moss, even with seven-league boots. The small village by the sea, where lived the Eskimos, was reeking with fish, filth, dogs, and children.

The traveller has only to go north to realize how great a part of life the fish are to the natives. As rice to the Chinese, lentils to the Egyptians, and meat to the Caucasians, so is fish – and fish means salmon – to the Eskimos.

At last, on July 6, in the early morn, a steamboat, black with people, came swiftly from the south, round the bend of the harbour. She touched at the rickety wharf, discharged her passengers at once, and then steamed directly across to the *St. Paul* in mid-channel. Tying up to the side of the big steamship, and connecting by some planks thrown across, we witnessed at first a stream of men coming on board, every one with heavy bags of gold-dust on his shoulders, or carrying between two of them small strong wooden boxes with iron straps.

Presently there came up from below on the steamboat boxes a little larger, heavily bound, each one tugged along by four men, who stumbled and tottered under the burden. This treasure was part of several millions now being transferred to the strongbox of the *St. Paul.* We new-comers looked at the bags and boxes gloatingly and admiringly, from the high black sides of the ocean vessel, as they came on board our steamer; and for myself, I thought that where so much came from there should be more left.

If gold existed in the Klondike, as this exhibition proved, then it was a fair chance for all, and I was quite willing to continue. After this we were all ardour and impatience to leave; and two days later this same steamer, the *Leah,* started on her return to Dawson. She had a large flat barge in front, 175 feet by 75 feet, the shallow hold filled with cargo, and the deck fitted up after a fashion with what served as sleeping berths and rooms. It was covered by a flat roof, with long tables set in the middle, at which 175 of us fed. The steamer *Leah* herself transported 125 more. Though primitive, the arrangement of the barge was not too rough or uncomfortable. The long, almost nightless days and relatively warm weather enticed every one outside to view the deep, swelling, wide, swiftly-moving river on its way to the sounding sea. So quiet and yet so strong, this river of the Far North seemed to dominate the whole land as well as those afloat upon its waters.

But all that was later, for our first day was decidedly unpleasant. In going down the sixty miles along the southern coast of Alaska that extends from St. Michaels to the upper mouth of the Yukon, we ran on a sand-bank while yet five miles distant from land. Yet neither the boat nor barge, loaded as they were, drew more than 4 feet of water. This was our first example of the power of the river in shallowing these seas. The wind blew off shore; the mist and rain came down and enveloped the vessels; the waves rocked the long and lightly-loaded barge, and the land became invisible. The women wept and wailed; and though the men knew it could be but 4 or 5 feet deep all the way to the shore, yet that shore was miles distant, and the waters were black and icy cold. All in all, it was a bleak and desolate outlook, and a very discouraging commencement of our last stage in the voyage to the Klondike.

A narrow channel of sufficient depth had been carefully staked, but our captain had drifted outside this channel on to the flats through ignorance or carelessness. There was a good deal of both in those earlier days up north, and men having no property of their own were not very careful of others'. We remained imbedded in the mud thirty hours. The barge impeded the boat, and was difficult to pull off. But finally at high tide we were once again afloat, and steamed on very slowly and cautiously, sending out canoes and finding the depth with poles every few minutes from the deck of the barge, which was ahead.

Gradually the channel became wider and deeper, and presently we swung round a bend into the turbid, whitish current of the dreaded yet desired Yukon River. At this one mouth it was two or three miles wide, and a whole forest of trees seemed to glide with its creamy current. The low alluvial delta was strewn with logs, timber, and smaller brush, like an upturned forest. Myriads of ducks and geese swam rapidly away from our approaching boat, not trying to fly. I saw many young ducklings and goslings only two or three weeks old following their parents, though it must have been a mile from shore. We made good headway, and soon passed a small river coming in from the north, up which, two or three miles from its entrance into the Yukon, were located the winter-quarters of the river steamers. The ice in the Yukon gives way earlier in the spring on the upper and lower ranges than at St. Michaels, so that boats stationed in this little stream can get away for the Klondike several weeks sooner than if they wintered at St. Michaels.

The next day we stopped two hours for wood – and mosquitoes. The former is cut by white men during the winter months, as close to the bank as possible, where the landing is good. The wood was mostly dry birch, spruce, and cedar, cut in four-foot lengths, split, and sold at about 8 dollars a cord. A "cord" of wood is a stack 4 feet by 4 by 8. Our boat burned a cord an hour, and averaged four miles during that period against a strong swelling current of five miles an hour. No one could swim up 10 yards against it, as we ascertained later.

A wonderful river dropping into the seas these countless ages unknown to civilized man!

The mosquitoes were frightfully hungry and decidedly audacious. How those poor woodchoppers endured them and lived I never knew. Doubtless they had become acclimatized, but I heard later of prospectors on the Koyukuk – a northern tributary of the Yukon – who had been forced to return hastily from an exploring journey by the myriads of these pests. Fortunately, they did not follow us to the middle of the river, where the boat usually steamed; and so we were safe, except when we stopped for wood or at some river station.

The supercargo of the *Leah* bought dogs for his company at various points, until he had gathered thirty or forty, at prices ranging from 20 to 50 dollars each, paid either in money or supplies. These were intended for winter travel on the Klondike, and they were mostly of the Malamute breed – that is, the native dog, said to be one quarter wolf, docile brutes to men, but always fighting each other. No two could be chained together, as they would quarrel over their food, and their sharp and wolf-like teeth cut like lances. I had seen at St. Michaels a dog severely bitten in the ear by another until the blood flowed, and instantly he was worried, bitten, and harried by other dogs until, if the Eskimo owner had not whipped them away, the wounded dog would have been killed. With all this leonine ferocity, I have never heard of the pure-bred Malamutes attacking their master, unless to dispute with him for food during the long, cold winter days and nights. Caches for provisions are placed high in the air on stilts, for the dogs would tear down any ordinary door or entrance if on the ground. In these summer days, however, they lay on the lower floor of the boat lethargically on their backs, rousing only when food was placed before them. They are vigorous and helpful only in cold weather. They are not hothouse dogs. Their food is dried and fresh fish, mostly salmon, the first of the run.

The Yukon River salmon are of a most magnificent variety. Bred in these coldest of waters, the meat is firm, clear and white. What is called the "king" salmon weighs very often 50 pounds, and has a carmine, or dark purple hue on the scales. The steamer steward bought these princely fish from the natives for 25 cents each. The Eskimos had several methods of catching them, but the oddest was by means of boards a foot wide and an inch thick, nailed together lengthwise in a triangular shape, resembling a long spout, and but little wider than a good-sized salmon. This was submerged in 5 feet of water a foot from the surface and 20 yards from the shore. The salmon swimming along the side of the shore, against the strong current, went straight into this simple trap and could not get back, as not one could turn, and those in the rear pressed on those in front.

We saw eighteen massive salmon taken from one of these spouts in a few minutes, and the Indians said they caught scores every day while the run continued. At Holy Cross Mission, an old Russian settlement, we observed how the natives live and prepare for the winter. The fish were running plentifully, and every Indian, even to the little children, was busy bringing them up from the bank, opening them and hanging them on the trees, or temporary scaffolds, or tops of huts and cabins – everywhere, in fact, where a salmon could be put out to dry – up and away from the dogs. These last had a fine feast from the offal, and lolled about in stolid content. The aroma was none of the most pleasant, for a fish village on the Yukon smells like shambles.

The run lasts about six weeks, and in that interval the natives must provide food for their families, including their dogs, until next season. Very few wild animals exist on this Lower Yukon, and, with the addition of geese and ducks, salmon is the only food that the country provides for its inhabitants. No grain is cultivated. The Indians buy flour and light supplies from the traders, paying in dogs and furs, for they trap all through the long winter.

The climate near the coast was foggy and lowering, but day after day we came to a clearer and sunnier atmosphere, though we went still further north as well as east, even into the Arctic Circle. The big barge, where more than half of us lived, had a level roof 10 feet high over its entire surface above the dining-room and berth-rooms, which made a most excellent promenade. Gradually we became acquainted with each other, and made and unfolded plans for the future. Some women also were of the party, who were going into the unknown with a fortitude and intrepidity that was admirable. The gold which we men were seeking they were seeking also – but vicariously, through husbands yet to be found. There were Mrs. Juliet and her piquante daughter Georgie, of good old Virginia stock, with no relatives but each other, and with impoverished fortunes; yet they were venturing into this cold frozen North as serenely as if for a holiday.

"Georgie," said I, one sparkling evening as we regarded the brilliant sunset, "what prompted you and your mother to start for the Klondike entirely alone and without acquaintance?"

"We had nowhere to go," she replied; "I've been on the stage, but would get no engagement this year. We had to live. I had read of the Klondike gold, and I said to mother, 'Let's go; we can take in washing if necessary.' But I don't expect to," she added with a laugh.

And she didn't, for she married one of the most successful miners, and, as Mrs. George Thornehill, accompanied by her husband and mother, spends her hours now in leisurely voyaging from San Francisco to Cairo. But that did not come for a couple of years later. There was also a Swedish party – a mother, son, daughter, and son-in-law.

They came from New York, and did laundry work on the barge for some of the other passengers. The mother, though quite fifty, was energetic and industrious. Afterwards she met and married an old-time prospector with plenty of money, and has her house in San Francisco. So it will be seen that there was hope for all, and success to some.

We had also Colonel Rice, an ex-U.S. senator from Arkansas, who was going to Dawson to open a law-office, and incidentally operate in mines. The old senator did not then know that he could not practise law in Canadian territory – a knowledge that he acquired in due time. He was quite affable, very susceptible to female attractions, and, I verily believe, if anyone with authority to marry people had been of our company, the ex-senator would have been a husband to at least two ladies, if that were indeed possible. He complained to me one day, saying that "one of his lady friends was always ill and asking him for a little drop of whisky." Whisky was sold for 10 dollars a bottle on the barge and boat just as soon as we left St. Michaels. It was our first foretaste of Klondike prices, and, oddly enough, perhaps because of its cost, everyone had a thirst, like the soldiers east of Suez. In these regions alcohol seems more palatable and less injurious than in lower latitudes. During my three years in the Klondike I met a number of men who habitually drank a bottle of Scotch every night, with no apparent ill effects. Especially was this true in the winter, when the cold was so excessive that the body continually required stimulants. Nor did they become really intoxicated, but always knew what they were saying and doing.

We had also, among our Argonauts seeking the unknown, two ladies of mental and physical altitude. One was Mrs. Hitchcock, the widow of a U.S. naval officer, and the other was Miss Van Buren, related, it was understood, to a former U.S. representative to Japan. They were making the voyage from Frisco together, with the strangest agglomeration of cargo that ever women's wits devised. Two gigantic Danish dogs, a tent that would entertain seventy-five people – as was later discovered when it was unfolded and set up at Dawson – a collection of pigeons and rare fowls, boxes and boxes of *pâté de foie gras*, truffles, pâtés of other kinds, sardines, olives farcies, several kinds of musical instruments, and a bowling-alley. Naturally, the freight on this stupendous aggregation of luxuries for an Arctic mining camp was more, much more, than the ladies had anticipated. Therefore there was contention, and as Mrs. Hitchcock, who was superior in command, possessed in addition to her other accomplishments a most undeniable temper and tongue, the captain and various passengers felt the quality of both in infinite variety. The lady was finally left to a corner of the barge alone in womanly supremacy, where, in her silent intervals, she wrote what afterwards appeared in the form of a book on the Klondike. The work, of 500 pages, was based on this voyage up the Yukon, supplemented, after her arrival, by a stay of two weeks in Dawson and the vicinity, while disposing of her numerous choice chattels in a cynical and capricious camp of miners.

The men adventurers were an epitome of the multitude assembled in the harbour of St. Michaels. There were some who had lost fortunes and hoped to regain them; some who never possessed means, and therefore were full of ardour; and a few whom the tide of life had cast as flotsam upon this mighty river, and for whom the future had neither hopes nor fears. A large proportion were miners who had come from South Africa, Montana, British Columbia, and other mining localities – young, healthy, stalwart. Penmen averred that wages were 15 dollars a day at the mines, and everyone was eager to fly to the Klondike. As the days passed quickly and quietly, we began to meet small parties in boats and canoes, who were drifting down the river to St. Michaels. The first boat we met was occupied by ten men, a Yukon stove, a couple of sacks of flour, beans, bacon, and sugar, with some canned evaporated potatoes and other vegetables. We thronged the nearest side of our vessel and hailed with, "What's the news from Dawson?" "Bad news," they replied; "cold winter, poor grub, no work, and hundreds starving. Go back, you fellers," they added, "where you came from!" This was both unexpected and disheartening. We did not reflect that, even if gold lay in heaps on the open sward free for all, some men would be penniless and complaining. Other boats followed, until one day we counted 111, carrying downward fully 500 men.

Many of these canoes could not approach near enough on the broad, rapid current of the Yukon for us to hail them, even if we had been so minded; but the cry came over the deep river, ringing again and again, as they passed: "Go back! go back! The Klondike is no good." It reminded me, in its dreariness, of the cry of Stanley's crew going down the Congo: "Sennenneh! Sennenneh! Sennenneh!" – the river of the Equator and the river of the North Pole both tingling with like sounds, in men's voices, of doubt and despondency.

Not a woman was in these boats, that in these long summer days, when the sun set at eleven and rose at one o'clock, with a long, lingering twilight of blue and amber in between, never stopped, but, floating with the current for over 100 miles daily, soon reached their destination by the sea. After this repeated greeting, some of our adventurous party became more doubtful and irresolute, and more than one took silent, solitary walks along the smooth esplanade of the barge's level roof.

If they must turn back from the Klondike, where next in the wide world could they go? And it promised so well at the outset, and the gold looked so good and inviting at St. Michaels! Surely there must be more hidden in the frozen recesses of these far Northern streams. These men that fled were cowards, weaklings, who dared not face a week's hardships or fatigue. Let them go back; it made more room for the new-comers.

So we looked up the bright, brilliant vistas of the river, with its steep hills and pleasant grassy valleys bordering both banks, and turned our thoughts resolutely forward to Dawson and the Future.

Where the Koyukuk – perhaps the largest of its affluents – joins the Yukon, we came to a party of twenty, including five women, who had arrived there direct from Boston a day or two previously. Their encampment was on the sandy beach, and was encumbered with articles, most of which were clearly unsuitable for such an expedition. A wagon where there were no horses; a plough where there was no ground to furrow; boxes of crackers, which were light and bulky, instead of flour; guns and ammunition where there was neither game nor enemies – nothing but mosquitoes, though of these abundance for all. We stayed by their camp a couple of hours, and before we left they were begging or buying tobacco from the passengers, being even then bare also of an article so essential and necessary to the miner as bacon. The Koyukuk, which they proposed to explore with a very small steam-launch, was then comparatively unknown, and stretched away to the northeast for over 800 miles, its sources being adjacent to the Arctic Ocean. Not one had ever been West before, and none seemed very capable.

In New England they had read in the newspaper press roseate tales of the millions of gold in these regions, and, tired with their barren, non-productive life, had made up a company – and here they were, without ever having had proper advice or taken intelligent action as to what they needed or where they were going.

I foresaw nothing but disaster and death, and, indeed, they seemed lonely and forlorn enough, sitting on their boxes and barrels, tormented by myriads of mosquitoes, and sadly watching our boat move away from the shore and into the river. The later occurrences can be shortly told.

After proceeding some distance up the Koyukuk, that river became too shallow for voyaging, while yet 200 miles from the reported gold-fields. The expedition then cached part of its supplies, and with the rest journeyed onward through the unexplored. The gold was not found in large quantities, and only the neighbouring creeks were prospected. Hill claims were unknown at that period. So the days passed without success until early winter came. A few remained, with little food, while the majority returned to the Yukon, leaving several weaklings on the trail who died of cold and starvation. The rest subsequently returned and wintered at Rampart, living on the bounty of the miners there, and in the spring scattered to Dawson or Tanana, or went back home.

I never heard of a single member of the party making even a partial success. One can do very little without proper knowledge and equipment.

A day or two longer, and we landed at the foot of the bluffs which located Rampart, a mining hamlet of a score of log cabins, each a single room, with one or two larger structures containing provisions and mining implements sold by traders. It was a brilliantly sunny day, and the tops of the birch-trees covering the level terrace beyond the high river-bank sparkled in the crisp transparent atmosphere. Over the plank, so soon as laid, came a number of men, gaunt, rough, and ragged, with wistful though healthful faces, and a great longing in their eyes.

Ours was the first boat up the river this summer. The foremost asked the passengers nearest him: "Did you bring any mail?" "Yes." "From New England?" "From everywhere, we think; ask the purser." But the latter was already on deck with a small package of letters. "What is your name?" he asked. "James Stapleton." The purser scanned the addresses while the miners stood, as did all of us, quiet as the waters that glided gently by the still boat.

"Here are two letters from Portland, Maine, for James Stapleton, Rampart, Yukon River," said the purser, giving them to the enraptured man. We almost cheered. His face was transfigured, as with uncertain steps he turned to leave.

"They are from my wife," he said simply. "This is July, 1898, and I have not heard a word from the folks since I left home in May of last year." And he went to his lonely cabin holding them in his hand. They would be opened and read when alone and unseen by curious eyes.

There are pathetic tales of this North land that will never be told.

At this point the river emerges from a noble series of steep hills guarding its waters on both sides. They extend along its course for 200 miles, and are so embattled in appearance as to give to this part of the country the appellation of Ramparts. For this entire distance the Yukon is half a mile wide, with rapid, smooth current, and deep enough to float an ocean liner. The colour is clearer than farther down, although it is never a pellucid stream, for the inflow of the White River near its sources above Dawson gives it a permanently creamy appearance. The White River, an affluent of fair volume, courses through volcanic lands, which so impregnate its waters with ashes and pumice that where it empties into the Yukon it actually looks not unlike soup. As a little milk colours a whole glass of water, so does this moderately large White River change the colour of the entire volume of the immense Yukon, even with its dozen or more tributaries coming from the eternal ice and snow of the North land, none of which is smaller than the White River. The swift water between the Ramparts made our daily advance less, especially as wood was scarce. These hills bear very little timber – at least, near the river-banks—though covered with a thin vegetation of grass. They were of granite formation, and overhung the deep channel to such a degree at several points that it was intensely interesting as we passed under the massive awning. This was a most beautiful portion of the voyage, and we remained on the roof of the barge from 5 A.M. until 10 P.M., except when eating.

Violin and mandolin music with dancing caused the hours to pass more lightly in their going. The sun was warm and pleasant, and its setting behind us as we proceeded eastward provided a number of rainbows, lasting for hours. For in this latitude, at this period of the year, it is fully two hours from the moment the sun dips below the horizon until the last glimmer of diversified colours is lost in the gray of the night. What chances and opportunities for a great landscape-painter!

The whole of the Yukon River in its primeval beauty has charms and attractions undescribed, unwritten, and unknown, for the savants and naturalists as well as the artists and hunters.

Emerging at last from this wide and noble pass between the mountains, we arrived at the Yukon Flats. For several hundred miles the river follows a sluggish course between islands and over shallows spreading out to a width of over forty miles. Originally this must have been a large lake, and its destruction was perhaps occasioned by the cutting of the passage through the hills which we had just left.

The channel, or what may be termed the channel, changes every spring, through the tearing and grinding of the ice when breaking up; so the Indian pilots who direct these boats always make a winter trip to the Flats, and note where the ice is thickest, for there will be the most likely channel for the coming summer.

Our progress was most tedious, the water being frequently but 3 feet deep under our heavy steamboat, and her least draught when loaded was 4 feet. Still, the mud was soft, and one way or another we pushed along. From the top of the mast one could not see even with glasses the northern or southern boundary. Yellow mud on the shallows, with low islands covered, or partially so, with young cottonwood-trees. Driftwood everywhere, all small, or at least not more than one or two years old, for the fearful freshets and the immense volume of water that comes roaring down the river in May and June carry heavy birch and spruce trees like chips in their progress. Still, some of the debris lodges here and there, and navigation will be yearly more difficult, eventually requiring Government aid to dredge a permanent channel, if that, indeed, be possible.

Abundance of water-fowl existed in the lagoons, and under the shadows of the trees on the islands' sandy surfaces, but no large game. Many of the brown bears which formerly roamed in this locality have been killed. Nor did the river contain many fish, other than salmon, which industriously swim up to the lakes 1,800 miles from the mouth of the Yukon. The thick, milky waters do not encourage the propagation of many other species. However, most of the larger tributaries of the Yukon are thronged with delicious fish, grayling being very numerous. They remain in the clear waters of their home streams, and do not descend to the river.

After clearing the shallows we passed by Circle City, the oldest mining town on the river, built about 1890. It was said to contain more cabins than people, for all that could had gone to Dawson ahead of the rush of which we were a fragment. So we proceeded onward, passing several smaller tributaries, but not finding the volume or force of the river much diminished.

At high noon, twenty-one days after we left St. Michaels, we tied up at the only wharf in Dawson, with 10,000 people on the banks loudly cheering our arrival, for we brought the mails and were the second boat that year arriving from civilization. It was July 27, and I had been forty-six days on my long voyage from San Francisco to that Dawson I so ardently longed to behold.

Chapter 2

FIRST DAY IN DAWSON

It was a brilliant July morning as we stepped on shore at Dawson. Back of the marsh and level land, covered with tents and rude cabins, rose sharp and sheer into the transparent air a huge mountain. Its steep sides were in places lightly covered with young birch and spruce trees and bushes; other portions were quite stony and without vegetation. On the muddy shores lay a long line of small boats extending fully a mile. They reminded me very much of the river boats at Canton. These Dawson boats had come down from the lakes after the ice had broken, carrying thousands of adventurous men and women, as well as quantities of supplies of all kinds. They had preceded us by some weeks, and were even then coming in by scores daily. These wanderers had passed the winter and early spring on Lakes Linderman and Bennett. At the last-named lake boats were constructed of a uniform size, each one carrying half a dozen people and a couple of tons freight quite comfortably. After the ice had broken, the boats rowed over Lake Bennett to its outlet, and thence dropped down to the beginning of the Yukon. From thence to Dawson was a pleasant voyage on a beautiful river, drifting with the current. It was only a week or ten days from Lake Bennett to Dawson.

Senator Rice and myself took a walk through the crowded street, crowded as the Strand or Broadway, and a mile long. There were no side-walks, and the narrow way was dusty where it was not crossed by pools of stagnant water.

"I'm rather disappointed," said the Colonel. "Why?" I asked.

"Well, I hardly know," he said. "I suppose in all ventures of this kind the first emotion on arrival is doubt and distrust. But it seems to me all these men should be at the mines, if there are any, and not be loafing around the saloons and the streets. And it isn't as big as I thought it would be, from all I had heard; in fact, I'm in a mood to return."

"What! without looking into things?" said I. "That will never do. Drinks are 50 cents, oranges a dollar each, meals 3 dollars, and a cot 2 dollars: we have learned all this in ten minutes. Where men spend money at these prices, there must be gold, and plenty of it. If there is, I'll take my chance with the others of getting some."

But the Colonel was dubious and despondent. He was old, he said, and never should have come. He could at least make a living elsewhere.

To my surprise, on returning to the boat, where we remained until evening, I found several others of his opinion. It was strange that men should sell property, break up homes, travel thousands of miles, braving all dangers and troubles with matured purpose, and then falter and become discouraged on the very threshold of their journey's end.

On the *Leah* with us was a French-Canadian Jesuit ecclesiastic called Rene. He was, I believe, the titular head of the various missions established in the Far North by his

Order. We had become well acquainted during the long voyage. He advised me at once not to stop on the flat, which was full of typhoid and dysentery.

"Better go up on the hillside and pitch your tent. You can eat anywhere. It's all equally bad and dear."

So, learning that there was ground behind the Catholic church, which was located on a high bluff overlooking the river, I asked Father Rene for permission to camp on his rocky boulders at the back of the church, which he readily granted. I bought a stove, cot, and mattress. I had a tent 8 by 10 feet, and a magnificent lynx robe, purchased in San Francisco, made of twenty-one lynx-skins, and the most serviceable garment I ever possessed.

After a frugal meal of beefsteak and evaporated potatoes, I descended to the town, which spread out loosely and irregularly over the whole marshy level to where the famed Klondike River loses its clear, pellucid waters in the milky stream of the Yukon. At 10 P.M. the sun was shining brightly, and the streets or street was as animated as at midday. Thousands of men and many women wandered aimlessly up and down the narrow thoroughfare or drifted into the saloons. Of these there were at least half a dozen larger than the rest, with wide-open portals, containing hundreds of people. Every one was pushing and jostling around the faro and roulette tables, some to play and some to see. A man sat in front of a huge pair of gold scales, and was ever busy in weighing, from the sacks of gold-dust handed him by the gamblers, quantities of dust in value from 50 to 1,000 dollars, for which he gave them ivory chips to bet with. Far back in the darkened rear were two or three violin-players, to whose violent music danced, or rather leaped, a number of men and women. These latter were all young, attractive, and with but few signs of dissipation. That would come later, for they were mostly young women who had drifted down with the tide to Dawson, and found no other way of existence. It was costly for women to live in those days, and there was little leisure for reflection or opportunity for returning. Unless a woman had means or relatives, the only resource was the dancing-hall, for no decent employment could be found in the shops except for a very few, and at this period the trails to the mines from Dawson were so execrable that only hardy, robust men could travel and carry sufficient food for even a few days. Morality is under some conditions of life a question merely of necessity and self-protection. Men who never before knew faro or roulette were betting largely and recklessly after a few days' stay in Dawson, before, in fact, they had penetrated to the mines or made any serious inquiries. The long voyage seemed to have sapped their principles, and the whole environment of the place was that of another and a worse world. It was all a game of chance, and perhaps the gambling tables would be as propitious as the mines.

A restless, seething throng poured in and out of the saloons and sauntered up and down the dusty street, while the rays of the late-setting sun glanced bright and brilliant against the white snow crowning the rocky slopes of the distant eastern mountains. Yet there was little drunkenness, and less boisterousness. Three-fourths of the multitude were Americans, and the Stars and Stripes hung placidly caressing the short masts of nearly all the boats along the eastern shores of the river. But I learned then, as later, that while the Canadian laws were no better than, nor indeed very much different from, our American laws, their execution was more stringent and energetic. Legal offences were punished, and not only punished, but punished promptly, which is the main thing. Lawyers were not permitted the same latitude to delay and hamper justice, and the magistrate exercised more authority than in the United States.

In Dawson at this period the magistrate was Captain Starnes, a Canadian with an Anglo-Saxon name and a French-Canadian ancestry. He was, perhaps, sometimes precipitate in his decisions, but never unjust, and, above all, always prompt. He was a Captain of the North-West Mounted Police, that admirable body which keeps guard over both Indians and whites. In uniform they patrolled the town, and under their surveillance it was as quiet and orderly as a New England hamlet. In fact, I was struck this evening, and ever afterwards, with the sober disposition of the people. The distance they had come and the uncertainty of the adventure had chastened the spirit. Men walked the long street, conversed of prospects and new discoveries, even drank and gambled, with sedate mien and little laughter. There was no flippancy or recklessness in their discourse, such as would be witnessed in similar American camps. It was not so easy to gain this weird city of the Arctic zone, and failure meant more than in lower latitudes. The dread severity of the coming winter was ever present to the mind, and the high prices of food and supplies forbade consolation to him that had a slender purse. Besides, the reports were not cheerful. There seemed to be too many men and too few mines. I was reminded of the croakings of the departing Klondikers, who had passed us on the river, and I wondered if they had been right, and if I ought to turn back also and go home; but I reflected that I had brought some money with me, that I had had some mining experiences, and therefore had some advantages, and that, at the worst, I could leave in September by the upper river route and get away before the freeze-up. So I retraced my steps to my tent on the rocky hillside above the church, with the cemetery just behind, and lay down on my cot while the midnight sunset was resplendent in its glories athwart the western horizon.

Chapter 3

THE POST-OFFICE

In the early morn I had finished my breakfast of beans, bacon, bread and coffee, and descended the rocky hill to the beach and level ground. The sun was indescribably brilliant, without too much warmth. There was not a cloud on the horizon, and the exuberant rays filled the sky. They were penetrating and life-giving, lifting up the flowers that bloomed on the hills around, and illuminating with radiant clearness the tents, the rude cabins, and the innumerable boats that all together constituted the Aladdin-like city of Dawson. For it was a city, not a hamlet nor a mere village, that fair morning, with its 25,000 young adventurers, voluntarily assembled from over the world. They were the forerunners of a new crusade, but it was the religion of Mammon, and not of God, that had impelled their steps and aspirations to these climes. The air was so buoyant, the atmosphere so transparent, that I seemed to walk without exertion or volition. I then experienced for the first time what I afterwards knew to be in truth a feeling of mental and physical energy which is unknown to other latitudes. It is part of existence here, and seems bound up with the climate and the free, unhampered life.

Down on the long and muddy beach was excitement and fascination. For a good mile on the curved shores, as far as one could see, there rested boats and rafts, many of these latter laden with 10 to 90 tons of merchandise. They were being unloaded by men in nondescript habiliments, but nearly all wearing high rubber boots, for the stern of the boats floated in a foot or two of water, while the prow nosed deep in the muddy beach. A very few horses were hauling the goods in wagons to various parts of the town. I wandered slowly to the extreme southern point, where the Klondike and Yukon joined, and then, leaving the busy shore, went inward a few yards to the still more busy streets. Everyone was working – no one idle. An auctioneer was selling distant mines with the aid of a map displayed to the new-comers who crowded his large tent; small open spaces in the street were piled with a most extensive assortment of everything under the sun, often labeled with the most fanciful prices; bread-makers were selling the warm white loaves made from Canadian flour, the best in the world, as fast as they came from the unprotected oven; while piles on piles of uncovered dry goods, provisions, and other supplies, lay in the open air. A storm of rain would do infinite damage, it occurred to me, but there was no shelter.

Men were building log cabins for shops and residences, but material was scarce, and the single small sawmill could not cope with the demand. I stopped at my banker's, and found the bank to be a tent, with an unplaned board for counter, and the clerks in their shirt-sleeves; while the safe was merely an old open trunk behind the unplaned board. For all that, I observed that the trunk held bags and bags of gold-dust, and that hundreds of thousands of dollars in currency lay carelessly about in ill-assorted piles. Miners came in, selling their gold-dust at the uniform ratio – 16 dollars per ounce, paid in gold coin or Canadian paper money — whilst traders were buying drafts payable for goods from the "outside." Interest was 10 per cent. per month for good private loans on mining and Dawson property, though the banks only charged 2 per cent. per month.

One can imagine, therefore, how high were the prices of commodities, and what must be the feverish hope of gain to pay such extraordinary rates of interest! I was more and more satisfied, and resolved to remain. Going to the *Leah*, which I knew would leave for St. Michaels in the afternoon, I met Wichter. Wichter and his wife were an old German couple who had sold their little grocery and beer store in Sacramento, and came to Dawson on our vessel. Mrs. Wichter must have weighed over 300 pounds. She was so obese that it was with difficulty she could walk, and most of her hours had been spent in her big chair, guarding, like a giantess, the entrance to her state-room. He was quite sixty, and not in very good health, yet these two had given up their home and ventured the savings of a lifetime to arrive at this uncertain whirlpool of the Klondike! He was talking with his wife, who still filled the big chair, only it was out on the deck. They looked disconsolate, and greeted me sadly.

"What are you going to do?" queried the old woman.

"Going to do?" I replied; "I don't exactly know, but there are plenty of chances. What will you do? Will you open a restaurant?" I continued.

Wichter looked me steadily in the face, and simply said: "We are returning home to Sacramento on the *Leah* this afternoon."

"Yes," added his wife; "I have not left the boat. From this upper deck I can see the town pretty well, and I am afraid. It's no place for us, with all these men and bad women. I don't know why we came here."

And she wept, while the old man said no more, but twisted his long, lean fingers pitifully. Back with them went a half a dozen more of the fainthearted. I hardly know why; perhaps they could not say themselves. Possibly they had expected to pick up gold in the streets of Dawson. Perhaps they were terrified by the thousands who had preceded them, and who yet had not gone to the mines. The tales told of the rigours of the fast-coming winter, with its fearful cold and isolation, may have appalled their spirits.

The Colonel and the ladies, with others of the passengers and myself, were at the wharf when the boat backed out and, turning swiftly in the current, vanished from view round the bluff below.

We retraced our steps to the town, and I addressed my thoughts to my future plans. In a few days I hired a new cabin, suitably located, divided into two rooms, for 100 dollars monthly, "unfurnished." I put in a cot, stove, table, and chairs, with some white lining over the bare log walls. I bought a console for my violin, and half a dozen cases of kerosene for my two lamps, which were to illuminate the cabin during the long, cold, dark winter nights. The stove was of the "Yukon" pattern, specially constructed for high latitudes. It was of thin sheet-iron, oval, with a damper in size and shape like a telescope, extending along the side from the top to the bottom. This gave a strong and speedy draught. The round cover was in the top, and blocks of wood a foot in diameter could easily be slipped within. The lightness of these stoves, combined with the quickness with which fire and heat could be obtained, made them very serviceable, though only the rudest kind of cooking could be done. For myself, I ate in the restaurants. The floor was covered with one or two old Turkish rugs that I bought at an auction, though later I put down some matting. Neither, as in weeks to come I knew, was sufficient to prevent the cold air from entering through the cracks in the floor between the boards made by the drying of the green-cut lumber. The logs that formed the sides and roof shrank only a little, and by filling up the interstices with more moss, the cement of the Yukon, I was able to keep those parts of the cabin fairly intact. The three windows – two in the front-room and one in the back-room – were double, with single sashes.

Many cabins had windows made of empty stout and ale bottles, set with the bottoms inward, giving a good enough light, and yet to some degree excluding the cold air. A window-sash holding six panes 6 inches by 6 inches sold in Dawson for 25 dollars! So only aristocrats or "cheechakas" – i.e., newcomers – indulged in such unnecessary luxuries. One of the advantages pointed out to me on hiring my cabin was its nearness to the "water-hole" in the river. I did not then know what that meant, but subsequently learned that in the winter, when everything was frozen, water was obtained by digging 4 or 5 feet through the ice on the Yukon to the stream which always runs below. Those in the vicinity dig the hole in common, and carry water away in buckets. Gradually the hole freezes from the bottom upward, and then another is excavated. It appears that it is never so cold as to freeze all the sources of water, and that plenty can usually be obtained by cutting through the ice. This also is true in a lesser degree of the smaller affluents of the Yukon, like the Klondike and the Stewart.

A week after my arrival I saw a great crowd at the principal street corner as I came down in the morning. A man clad in a dirty red shirt and high rubber boots stood on a wagon, and in loud, clear, and penetrating tones read, from a newspaper that had just arrived from up-river, an account of the battle and capture of Santiago. The throng cheered and cheered, and men whose faces had suffered no smile to be visible on them for days clasped hands with those standing near, while someone struck up "Marching through Georgia." To my surprise, the Britishers present, who were quite as demonstrative as the Americans, joined in the song, and appeared to know its music quite as well as my own countrymen. Afterwards I knew that the melody is an old English refrain.

The reader of the war extract, after finishing its perusal, announced that the rest of the paper would be read aloud in a hall near by – admittance 1 dollar! In fifteen minutes the place was thronged at that price with 500 men, who patiently stood for over an hour while the enterprising owner read to them accidents, suicides, telegrams, advertisements, and all that go to make up the life of a Vancouver daily newspaper. For three weeks not one recent paper had appeared in Dawson, and in our sudden isolation the craving for news was as the craving for food. We had something besides mines to talk about for the rest of the day.

The next morning the mail, of which the paper had been the private precursor, arrived from the States and Canada. A line was formed in the afternoon extending 100 yards down the dusty street from the log-cabin post-office. The line was kept at an unvarying length by the constant arrival of miners who, hearing on the creeks that a mail had arrived, dropped pick and shovel, and hastened to Dawson with the hope of receiving letters from the loved ones at home. The post-office arrangements for delivery and distribution were abominable in those early days.

Ignorant and incompetent clerks delivered letters to the eager, anxious applicants from the two little windows in a slow and exasperating manner.

"Is there not a letter for me – James Culverhouse?"

"No."

"But I am sure there must be one," said the explorer in an appealing voice.

"I tell you there ain't any; move away and give another man a chance," said the official.

The miner started to leave with a dejected countenance, but as the clerk was putting a hunch of dirty letters back into the little receptacle marked "C" the man cried:

"Why, there it is! there it is! – the first letter in your hand. Don't I know my wife's handwriting?" he almost shouted in his excitement. "Give it to me right away."

The employee, almost grudgingly and without excuses, gave the applicant the letter that otherwise he might never have seen again. Many instances of this character are said to have occurred.

The day after, the line remained unshortened. A heavily-bearded giant from Dominion Creek called out to a slight man, the fifteenth ahead:

"What will you take for your place in the line, pard?"

"Twenty dollars," was the prompt reply.

"All right, here's the cheese;" and they changed places.

It brought the big man that much nearer to home.

There were no papers – only letters were brought down by the mail contractors; but newspapers, carried on the boats by private passengers, sold readily in Dawson for a dollar each. In two or three days they were collected again, sent up the creeks, and resold for 50 cents each, because they were a few days old in the Klondike. All were disposed of, and the bringing in of newspapers became quite an enterprise that fall and winter. When I bought a San Francisco paper for a dollar it was delightful revelry for the whole evening. I began at the first page, and read every line, advertisements and all, and so on to the last word of the last line of the last page. Nothing escaped me, and I was therefore better informed of the doings of the world, for that day at least, than anyone in Frisco. I learned of businesses and affairs that I never knew before to have existed; and it was a pleasant remembrance, when I returned three years later, to recognise, from their advertisements, places and establishments that seemed to be old and familiar friends.

Chapter 4

TRIP TO FRENCH HILL

After six o'clock every evening people walked from Dawson to the different creeks, not one of which was distant more than thirty miles. They were loaded according to strength and purse; and as darkness, or even twilight, came not before midnight, it was more agreeable to walk the marshy miles in the cool setting evening sun than in the hot, dusty afternoon.

Ten days after my arrival I left Dawson for my first trip to the mines. My destination was Eldorado Creek, fifteen miles away. With two other men I started at 5 p.m., eager to see at last the gold actually taken from the ground. But I almost regretted my journey. I had lived a careless club-life in San Francisco for years, and was not, therefore, very hardy, though strong and with good constitution. From the moment we crossed the Klondike on a rickety ferry, two miles from Dawson, we plunged into a mire of muddy water and detachments of dark moss about a foot in diameter, lifting their heads just above the water or marshy subsoil. The business was to step from one tuft to another, and, though close enough together, they were soft and slippery. To miss sent one down to the knees or hips in Arctic mud and water. Through superior wisdom or ignorance I wore Frisco light shoes, not having yet fitted myself with rubber hip-boots in Dawson. One can imagine my plight with these varnished shoes and trousers to match, the whole costume being that of a fool, and not a miner nor a would-be miner. Draggled and wretched I sat me down to rest at No. 60, Bonanza, the halfway roadhouse, and watched the loaded miners walk silently and steadily by and onward. People do not seem to talk or laugh much in this country. Life is too serious, and they are too far from home and friends.

One man had strapped to his back two sacks of flour, weighing together 100 pounds. Another carried a sack of flour, a small Yukon stove with two lengths of pipe, some bacon, coffee, sugar, a pick, shovel, axe, pan, and a pair of blankets. He was equipped for any emergency, and looked like a small branching tree. I thought that, if these men could not command success, they did more – they deserved it. To see them stalking ahead uncomplainingly under their Titanic loads, while I fretted and worried with nothing but myself to transport, made me ashamed of my weakness; and I sprang up and started ahead with vigour and energy. Example is better than precept.

By midnight we arrived at the Grand Forks, a small hamlet at the junction of Bonanza and Eldorado Creeks, two of the principal gold-bearing streams. After a good and plentiful supper we went to the blanket cots that were offered as beds. Whoever had occupied the blanket before me had forgotten to remove his boots; moreover, he had reversed his position and slept with his feet where his head should have been. As a result I found the head of the bed ornamented with globules of dried mud of varying size and appearance, which adhered firmly to the black blanket – I know not if it ever had any other colour. I was so excessively fatigued, especially in the legs – from pulling them out and letting them down in the marsh when they slipped off the moss tufts – that I could not rest. I kept pulling them up and letting them down mechanically, while the strains of an old fiddle and older voice, mingled with the shuffling noise of half-drunken men and women dancing in the room below, assisted in keeping me awake during the process. My first night in the mines is not alluring to recall.

By six we were astir, and, descending the rickety stairs, found a good breakfast of coffee, beefsteak, and evaporated potatoes. The sun was brilliant overhead, and, despite my fatigue, I felt a buoyancy and exhilaration that were delightful. All Nature looked serene as we commenced a brisk walk up Eldorado. In an hour or two we reached our journey's end, and I at once began, aided by a couple of men with picks and shovels, to examine the mine which I had come to visit. I had had some previous experience with mines in Nevada and California, though not of a very extended nature. However, before the forenoon was passed I satisfied myself that the mine was practically exhausted, and therefore so said and acted. I may add that this same fall the property was sold to a "cheechaka" (new-comer) for 5,000 dollars, all of which, together with subsequent expenses, he lost. Many persons, through ignorance and lack of sufficient inquiry, invested in mining properties which in some cases were entirely valueless.

After a hearty luncheon of bacon, coffee, and beans, with white, soft bread, Mr. Rogers and myself ascended French Hill to see the rocking process in the mines that, oddly enough, were there found on the very summit. I was introduced by Mr. Rogers to Mr. Templeton, a heavy, dark, keen-eyed man. He smoked a cigar which I knew must have cost a dollar, and with bare arms worked a rocker, while two other men brought dirt in barrows, and also buckets of water to replenish the small tub in which the rocker was placed. Templeton looked at me suspiciously as I gazed about inquiringly at the half-dozen men in their heavy rubber boots, who were digging the red dirt out from a cleared space beneath their feet, and washing it in a second rocker. "Who is this Lynch?" he asked Rogers in a low tone.

"Oh, he is a cheechaka from Frisco who has just come in. He is looking over the country to invest, and has some money. Let him see what you are doing. He'll say nothing to the officers."

And then I understood. The 10 per cent. royalty on gross output was not always paid to the Crown, and spies were about. On hearing that I came from San Francisco, he shook me cordially by the hand once more, and lifted up the top of his rocker, underneath being the gold, in size from minute particles to lumps weighing as much as 10 dollars. He took from his pocket a piece which he said weighed 55 dollars, that he had found in the rocker half an hour previously.

"How much have you there?" I asked, pointing to the rocker.

"Well, I should calculate about 500 dollars," he replied.

"For three men?"

"For myself and these two men since morning. The dirt is running kind of poorly to-day. But come into the cabin, and I'll show you something."

We three – Rogers, Templeton, and myself – went to the cabin, a short distance away, and I noticed that, though the door was closed, it was not locked, and, in fact, there was no lock. Locks were never thought of in the beginning of the Klondike era, and were not included in the miner's outfit. The cabin was roughly constructed of unhewn logs, and the uneven floor supported a narrow cot, on which lay a pair of dirty blankets. The little Yukon stove was covered with grease, and the table, made from a couple of unplaned planks, was littered with unclean and unwashed tinware dishes. A couple of home-made stools completed the meagre furnishing, but on an old shelf rested boxes of cigars that cost a dollar each in Dawson, and in the corner was a keg of Scotch whisky worth 50 dollars a gallon. Templeton, after giving us a drink and a cigar, opened an unlocked cupboard, and said, "What do you think of these?" removing and placing on the frail table three buckskin bags full of dust. "What do you think of this?" he added, reaching under the bed and placing upon the table one of those tin boxes which originally contain 5 pounds of ground coffee: 50 pounds of gold-dust now filled the same receptacle. "And what do you think of that?" he continued, going to a corner behind the door and removing an old gunny sack, covering a five-gallon can that once contained kerosene. "Come and help me," he added with a chuckle.

It took both of us to place it on the table beside the other golden treasures. It was two-thirds full, and must have weighed over 200 pounds.

"How much have you?" Rogers asked. "I think about 75,000 dollars." "How long have you been at work?"

"Four months – with three men at first, but now I hire six men, as you saw. I expect to take out 50,000 dollars more before it freezes in September, but then the mine will be pretty well worked out. It is only 100 feet square."

"What did it cost you?"

"Nothing," he said, with a smile. "Located it last April, and began work at once."

Seventy-five thousand dollars in four months, with 50,000 dollars more in sight, from nothing! Verily, this must be the haven for poor men!

I looked at the yellow gold lying in heaps in the two cans, fascinated and dreaming, while Templeton showed natural exultation, being now as frank as at first he was secretive. Men are not prone to conceal good-fortune. He had no education, and never possessed a thousand dollars before, so he deserved his success for braving this unknown and distant sphere.

He invited us to lunch, but a second glance at the dishes caused me to decline, though I highly respected his uncultured hospitality.

He went back to the rocker, smoking a fresh dollar cigar, whilst we descended the hill to Eldorado Creek below. Though it was late, yet my tired feeling was gone, and rather than spend another night with the mud blankets at the Grand Forks Hotel, I continued on the trail to Dawson, where we arrived late.

I was satisfied with my journey. I had lost one mine, but found there were others. Besides, the trip had tested my strength, and I was quite contented with the result. I slept soundly and well, dreaming of the cans and bags of gold on the miner's table, encompassed by the dirty dishes, with the single dirty window and the single lockless door.

Chapter 5

AUTUMN OF 1898 – DAWSON

After my return from the Eldorado trip, it occurred to me that my knowledge of mines was not yet sufficient to venture on my own judgment. So I thought it better to remain in Dawson yet awhile and gradually learn. Therefore I looked round for something to do in the town. A large shipment of provisions had arrived front St. Michaels, and the consignees refused to accept delivery through some fault in the contract.

The steamer that brought the goods to Dawson was not paid for its freight until a bank advanced the money and held the articles as security. These latter were piled upon the frail wooden wharf and on the dry sand at the back of the landing. They were offered for sale in blocks, but the regular trading companies, having their own boats and supplies, refused to purchase at any price. Besides, they wanted to discourage independent shipments. Money was scarce, and could be lent at 10 per cent. monthly, so purchasers were not numerous.

Finally I bought all the flour – 5,000 fifty-pound sacks – at 5 dollars per sack. The store price was 8 dollars, so it seemed a good margin. But when I took possession of my flour and looked around, I found no warehouse to store it, and no one to buy it, while the great pile was lying on the sand, covered with old tarpaulins and exposed to rain and thieves. The latter I guarded against by hiring a man during the day and another in the night – twelve hours each – at a dollar an hour. But the rain would come, and presently the snow; it was becoming colder daily. I was in a predicament, and wished I had thought longer before coming to Dawson, or at least, had reflected what I was to do with this particular lot of flour before, and not after, the transaction. I would go and look at the sacks on the beach very near the muddy shore, with its dollar-an-hour guard, and then go away making remarks to myself and of myself. After several days of this charming experience, I met Judge Wood, of Seattle. He had ground, but no storehouse; I could build the storehouse, but had no ground. So we came to terms. His land was a block from the main-street, in the centre of a marsh – in fact, it was the marsh. But it would be safe when the fire came – that inevitable fire which in their incipiency assails all mining towns. A road, therefore, was made through the marsh, at a cost of 500 dollars though only 250 feet long.

People were amused that I should build so far away, but no insurance could be obtained, and I was resolved to take no chances. I did not go to the Klondike to be burnt out. After a fortnight the storehouse was fairly complete, and the road not so very bad. Then came the transporting of the precious flour. The hire of two horses and wagon with driver ranged from 75 to 100 dollars daily. Feed was 30 cents a pound, and horses, even the poorest, 600 to 700 dollars. So, not to pay all my remaining funds to teamsters, I purchased a couple of teams and hauled it myself. Therefore in a month, instead of being, as I expected, a free, independent miner, I found myself only a common plebeian warehouseman, with a lot of stuff to sell and no one to buy: for I had only flour, and miners wanted other articles besides. But in this land everything moves quickly. The land is so distant and the summers so short that men decide affairs boldly and rapidly. I soon saw that I must combine different supplies with my flour to do any business. The people who had sold the flour had other provisions for sale also belonging to the same consignment. So I bought all their rice, beans, bacon, and rolled oats.

These I moved into the storehouse, and, finding that there was still some space unoccupied, I lent money at 5 per cent. and 10 per cent. monthly on merchandise to people who would store it with me. Very soon the warehouse was nearly full, and, with the assistance of an old man whom I hired as porter, I was kept quite busy all the day long. Of course there was no insurance, and all my belongings were inside these frail walls; but I could do nothing more. It was strange that, in a land commonly consecrated to ice and snow, fire was the danger to be feared and guarded against. The long, continuous summer dried out the green logs, and the fierce heat necessary in the winter stoves burnt through the thin iron pipes. The atmosphere in winter, though extraordinarily cold, was dry; and, with the snow piled 5 feet high against the walls, a spark from the worn-out chimney striking the mossy roof would kindle a blaze that enwrapped the house as if it were constructed of shavings. There was always a little bit of the gravel and moss roof cleared from the snow round the chimneytop by the heat, and the moss, thoroughly dried, was doubly dangerous.

The days gradually waned and the nights grew longer and colder. On September 14, 1898, fell in Dawson the first snow. It aroused the people to still more marvelous activity. The next day a long line of miners direct from the mines stood at the counters of the Alaska Commercial Company ordering winter supplies. Provisions for the whole winter were purchased in September, and payment made, in most cases at least, during May and June of the next year, when the melting of the ice enabled the miners to wash the gold from the dirt extracted during the winter, if it was there.

Each afternoon numbers of men with heavy packs left Dawson, going up the steep sheer hillside and down on the eastern slope, where lay the Klondike River ferry. A few had dogs, and still fewer horses. Each animal, human or quadruped, was weighted to its full strength. There were no drones in the Klondike. It was no sanatorium for the weary and faint-hearted. The thought that something must be done, something must be dared, for the time and money dissipated in the long and anxious journey to this Far North land was ever present. Each day arrived straggling adventurers, who had been on the trail a year, and sometimes longer, Canadians mostly, coining by way of the Porcupine or over the Great Lakes, who had wintered en route. Living by the gun and rod, for provisions were long exhausted, they appeared in Dawson hatless, shoeless, penniless, but yet not hopeless. They were breezy, cheerful, stalwart fellows, who thought the long journey well repaid by reaching the goal. To-day they arrived in Dawson; to-morrow saw them ten or fifteen miles up the creeks, sturdily looking for work in the mines, which was readily accorded. They were of the class of men who had opened the British North-West, and who will yet make an empire of that vast unpopulated region. For they are pioneers and builders, a large proportion being French-Canadian, or Canayens.

The nights grew sharper, and soon came the morning frost; the sun's rays, even yet bright, were weaker in the hazy sky. The days shortened with astonishing celerity, and we began to have a foretaste of what an Arctic winter day meant. Small ice-floes came slowly floating down the river; on the creeks, we were told, the streams were frozen. The leaves on the trees seemed to change colour daily, so rapidly did the keen though sunny atmosphere temper their beauty. The ferns and flowers on the hillsides drooped and withered. They had been glowing like a Scottish heath, which, indeed, the Klondike very much resembles in autumn. The ferns were of numerous species and enchanting, with long, wide, delicate leaves and branches.

Birds began to disappear, and the long flight of ducks and geese to the South began. The variety of birds most numerous was the small red robin, that sang and twittered from every bush and was not at all wild. Like the pigeons in Venice, they were everywhere in Dawson, fighting in the street over a grain of fallen corn. The following winter, when I lived in my chalet at the mine, they would come boldly in at the open door and peck around and about until I moved from the chair. Hunger made them gentle.

The ground became crisp underfoot, and leather soles were slippery. One day, walking through the street, I saw a man digging a hole with a heavy iron crowbar. The hole was about 5 feet deep. I stopped. "What are you sinking for?" I asked. "For a telephone-pole," the man replied.

"But why don't you use a pick instead of that heavy crowbar?"

"Because the ground is frozen."

"What! frozen that near the surface?"

"Yes, and a pick would have no more effect than a stick. Look;" and he struck the point of the crowbar against the black, flinty-like earth.

Sparks flew from the contact. The man added: "In ten minutes I will have to get the point of the crowbar hardened again by a blacksmith. This frozen gravel is harder than the hardest granite."

And I then realized that 4 feet from the ground the Yukon district was frozen hundreds of feet thick, through the action of hundreds of past centuries. It was with a measure of awe for Nature's illimitable powers that I realized how cold it must have been, and doubtless was even yet, so near to the North Pole.

But the days became shorter and the ice in the river increased. The last boat had left for down the river long ago, and on September 22 the last boat left for the "outside" via the Lakes and Skagway. It was a cold, gloomy, forlorn day. Cakes of ice thronged the fast-failing current, and people under heavy overcoats were shivering in the bleak air.

Her decks were crowded with all the faint-hearted who had not gone before, as well as with the belated in business. She bore on her limited area hundreds of passengers, and many of us who remained secretly regretted that we were not of their number, for the future of the winter looked very bleak and desolate in the long cold days to come, shut out as we were from the world by 600 miles of ice and snow, a wall so thick that it could not be penetrated for weeks. And there was no telegraph, and only sporadic mail communication by the aid of dogs. We did not know then that horses could exist in that severe winter temperature. Later we learned that horses can live wherever man lives, and live on what man lives on.

Judge Wood, who had established a flourishing business in furnishing supplies of all kinds to the miners, was on the boat. I looked at him wistfully. I had learned to know and to love the man. Formerly a Mayor of Seattle, with, it was stated, socialistic tendencies, I found him one of those in this oasis of the Northern ice-fields who had no vices. In the latitude of 63° – 'and yet no law of God or man ran north of 53°' – he neither drank nor swore nor debauched. Purely as a Vestal virgin, uprightly as a Cincinnatus, he lived in the Klondike, amid the all-pervading saturnalia which existed – at least in the town. He would walk miles upon miles on those slender steel legs of his, and dine frugally with a cup of water in some miner's dirty cabin; then lie down on the dirtier floor and sleep tranquilly until morn. I was sorry to see him go. But he had remained until the very last; and even then it was a question if he would not be caught in the fast-freezing river.

"You stay," he said, turning to me. "You have grit, mining knowledge, health, and some money. Stay. I have a family at Seattle, and must go out. But you should remain. Study the country, and you'll find a mine yet that will make you independent for life. It's worth while to spend a couple of years here, if the world is one's home thereafter."

Yet, withal, when the boat turned the corner of the bluff above the town and disappeared from view, I looked at the yellow river, shining with large and small blocks of ice floating in its cold, bleak, dead-coloured waters, and almost wished I had not come, or at least that, having come, I had gone. Even in the prisons of the world, only the walls separate one from the streets and life of the multitude. But here we were 600 miles from the nearest port on the sea, from the telegraph which could bring knowledge of outer existence; and every foot of those 600 miles would be soon covered with an icy and snowy wall, almost impossible to penetrate or surmount. And, after all, one might be unsuccessful – and then? "Better fifty years of Europe than a cycle of Cathay."

But those thoughts did no good. What was done was done. I was here, and here I had elected to remain. If there were gold, I believed I would get my share, and that it would be enough to repay me for the effort. If not, why then I should have deserved success if I had not succeeded. So I ate a good dinner at the only decent restaurant, and squandered the evening in the dancing-houses, where I ordered several bottles of champagne, at 15 dollars a pint, for the gaudy and slightly-dressed houris who favoured me with a dance and a *tête-a-tête* in the private boxes. They were numerous, young, and beautiful. From over the whole globe they had flocked to Dawson, for the fame of the Klondike treasures had overspread the world. All classes of beauties from all nations, but beauties all.

Some had a history and some not before they came, but all had a history after arrival. There was no honest occupation for women. Many went professedly as housekeepers to miners who were rich enough to employ one; but it was only another name. A very few found precarious and unremunerative employment in the stores, and the others drifted into houses kept for dancing, with gambling at faro and roulette as a principal adjunct. Those who could, danced and played; those who could not, assisted as *claqueuses*. But, withal, prizes were distributed quite impartially by fortune in the shape of rich mining husbands, and more than a dozen of these same dancing-hall girls are to-day enjoying married happiness at London, Paris, New York, and other places. And I make no doubt that they are quite as moral as the traditional Becky Sharpe. I know more than one case where the lady has reformed her dissipated husband, and keeps him in good strong leading-strings, to the edification of everyone who has witnessed a glimpse of the Klondike past. Those who have lived and are not altogether lost make excellent exemplars of virtue. Of good women there were few; of bad women plenty. So your lucky miner with cans of gold in his dilapidated cabin, pining in the cold winter days for women's society, dropped down to Dawson, into the music-halls, and engaged – a housekeeper. The housekeeper soon became a wife if she handled the gentleman rightly.

Of course, most of these men, while loyal good fellows of character and rectitude, would scarcely be taken for college graduates. They had led a desultory wandering existence in the North and North-West for years, and when the Klondike granted them sudden and abounding wealth, it was a Fortunatus's purse. They were amazed, if not abashed. So, from riding on horseback into Dawson saloons, smashing the mirrors and glasses and furniture, and paying thousands of dollars damages therefor without a murmur, to marrying ladies of questionable type and career, it was only a natural step. Gambling and drinking relieved them of some of their metallic burden; but yet I can recall few instances of men who dug a fairly good fortune out of the Klondike's ice-cold glens and glades and lost it in that manner. The gold was too difficult to get to be squandered recklessly. We were philosophers in the midst of our toils, and of our vices also. The gambling and dance halls did not capture all.

In the meantime the weather was dry, cold, and crisp. The sunshine, instead of being clear and bright, as in the autumn, became hazy and yellow. There was no rain nor fog, but the atmosphere was thick and gray in colour, and the tempered sunshine did not convey the heat or warmth of earlier days. The same could be equally said of lower latitudes, but yet it was different. The days shortened with appalling rapidity. I believe the sun at one time set seven minutes earlier each day. Unfallen snowflakes were for ever in the air, and the chill wind that came up the river pierced through cloth folds like arrows. Early in November it grew suddenly very cold, accompanied by fog, especially on the river, which by now had frozen over. One morning, when I arose in the cold dark room, I found my beard attached to my lynx robe by icy chains, and it was with some pain that I separated them. Then I knew why it was that men in the North land wear no beards in winter. That same day I had mine removed. After bathing and dressing, I walked by the river-bank as usual to my office. In the grayish mist that arose from near a water-hole in the ice, I dimly discerned winged black creatures which swept darkly above the whitish ice of the river surface. I stopped and looked with surprise and awe. Presently they landed on the ice, looking in the weird foggy atmosphere like gigantic black ostriches. A closer look, and I knew them to be ravens, of a larger size than any I had ever seen before. Poe's raven arose from the recesses of my memory, and I turned from these fantastical phantoms of the river to the life of the town. I observed several men in a group at the nearest street corner encompassed with fog smoke, while apart from them it was clear enough. It was only the congealing of the moisture of their breath in conversing. Similarly, I learned that on the coldest days the fog was most dense.

There were small places in the river near the shore where perhaps some spring kept the water from freezing. In the coldest weather – 50° below zero, for example – the moisture of the air in contact with the pool of water caused condensation and consequent fog. These air-holes, so to speak, on the river are quite numerous, and therefore it is as if one were in the midst of a November fog in London. We were told that during the low temperatures evidenced by these mists the Indians never travel, but remain stolidly within their huts or double tents. I say double tents, for it appears that if two tents are erected, one inside the other, with a space of perhaps 6 inches between, they are nearly, if not quite, as warm as a log cabin. The space between the tents becomes filled with ice and frost, with sawdust as an auxiliary, which seems to act as a buffer, and prevents the cold air from penetrating within the inner tent. On those extreme days there is no wind, which is providential, or it would be impossible for anyone travelling to survive, as 20° below zero with wind is regarded as quite as severe as 50° below in a tranquil atmosphere. A candle has been frequently lighted in severe cold and left outside, where it burnt until extinguished in the socket; this indicates how still was the atmosphere.

Meanwhile, life in the mines grew more quiet, and life in the town more noisy – at least, more thronged, for your Klondiker is not boisterous. He amuses himself for all that. Those who had gone to the mining districts looking at least for temporary employment returned to Dawson, for they found none. The miners who would have permanent employment during the winter, or at least the earlier part of it, until the mines were more opened, were already engaged, and there was no present occasion for others. I was astonished at the multitude that filled the ample gambling and billiard establishments every afternoon and night. For the sun was gone at 3 P.M., and the air, though clear, was ever crisp and Arctic.

These places had improvised most excellent stoves out of the iron barrels that carried kerosene oil to the Klondike. Emptied of their 100 gallons of oil, and standing on end, a log 4 feet long and 2 feet in diameter could easily be slipped in at the opened top. The draught through the several pipes that ran from the centre one to the corners of the large room was strong and persistent, and the double doors containing the vestibule kept the heat in.

Here was a smoking, drinking, gambling crowd of men mingled with gaudily-dressed girls dancing in the rear and drinking at the front. It was very close, and yet the keen icy frost outside was so penetrating that, even though the double doors were opened but for an instant for someone going or coming, the air of the place was not at all uncomfortable, despite the fierce and vivid heat from the giant stove. A dozen large lamps, each of which consumed a gallon of oil every twelve hours, gave a fairly good light, not much clearer, however, than the marvelous stars and the still more marvelous Aurora Borealis outside, lighting up the heavens from horizon to horizon with many-coloured hues. After midnight, those who had cabins went to them over the ice trail reluctantly and shiveringly, those who had not slept on and under the billiard-tables, leaving narrow passages along the sides through which men could walk.

These had no other home, nor could the town provide one, so perforce they lived thus, eating where and when they could and might. For the winter had brought destitution to many who had remained, and the authorities found it necessary to provide work for those who needed sustenance.

This labour was mainly employed on the "wood pile." In the several Government buildings immense quantities of wood were consumed, and at this period men were hired to do the work of cutting. But later the wise men who ruled found a better and a cheaper method. If a man was sentenced to gaol for a number of days for some offence, these thrifty Canadians did not let him pine alone and moody in his silent cell. Oh no! They brought him forth, put a saw into his bands, and set him to cutting wood. He was not solitary, for all the other prisoners were his companions, guarded by armed sentries pacing to and fro. Sawing wood around about 50° below zero, was no sinecure, and the fear of it prevented the commission of many a crime, for the culprit knew that conviction meant a sturdy and unremitting task on the everlasting "wood pile."

Chapter 6

MY FIRST SNOW EXPERIENCE

On November 16 the thermometer dropped 25° lower than the day before. It happened in the night. In the morning I awoke shivering with an icy tremor, though covered with a heavy lynx robe, which is the costliest, and therefore ought to be the best. Still, Nature has provided, it seems to me, equally good winter covering to all the wild animals that range the rivers and mountains of the Arctic regions. Lynx, marten, musk-rat, rabbit, bear, moose, and reindeer skins lessen in value downwards as I have enumerated them, yet they all appear to be equally serviceable. Even the Alaskan and Siberian dog robes, which are composed of half a dozen skins, and valued at only 20 dollars for each robe, are practically as warm as the lynx robe that, made of the same number of skins, is rated cheap at 100 dollars. None of these, however, seemed sufficient in this dreadful cold – 46° below zero – that now enveloped us as in a cloud. When I sprang out of bed and looked at the glass, it was 20° below zero in this cabin of mine, with its walls of thick logs, its floor and roof double, and the spaces between filled with 3 inches of sawdust, said to be the best armour yet found to battle with the enemy frost. Icicles an inch long hung to my beard and moustache, and had fastened themselves to the robe, the end of which fell below my mouth. Afterwards I learned to cover my head completely with the robe, like an Indian, and sleep semi-stifled during this excessively cold weather, for otherwise the robe accompanied me when I left the cot.

I lighted a fire. The wood, frozen through and through, split under the axe, and with the aid of a little kerosene shot up in a fierce yet comforting blaze. Everything was frozen to the spot where it had been placed – sponge, soap, towel, tooth-brush, shaving-brush, glasses, and bath-tub. After I had melted the pail of ice on the "air-tight" stove, I poured some of the water 2 inches deep into the bath-tub, which I had removed to the rear room, where there was no heat. Not two minutes had elapsed before I threw off my chamois pyjamas in the front-room, and, opening the communicating door, stepped hurriedly into the bath-tub, for I had no time to lose. Quick as I had been, the atmosphere had been quicker, and just as I stepped into the tub with both feet, wrenching, with a great effort, the soap from a beam hard by, I slipped on the newly-frozen ice in the tub, and over we went, soap, tub, myself, and several other utilities, all separated in different quarters of the room. Those two minutes had sufficed to transmute my water into smooth and glassy ice.

In an hour or so I was warmly clothed, and ventured forth to see and feel what it was to walk and breathe in the open air at 50° below zero. I observed at once from the little elevation on which I lived, above the town, that Dawson seemed on fire – at least, the smoke filled the streets, the atmosphere above, and even the wide expanse of the frozen river, until the other bank was invisible. I descended and overtook several men; they all walked fast, but I ran. It was more comfortable, if not so decorous.

"Where is the fire?" I asked.

One of them looked at me through his visor – for his face was covered with fur as with a helmet – and said, blowing a cloud of steam into my eyes from his nose and mouth:

"Can't you see it is the cold, you damned cheechaka!"

And I saw that it was so, for the smoke or steam was everywhere – on the river, the streets, the houses, until the ebon ravens, quarrelling with the dogs on the river ice for meat bones thrown away, resembled in the uncertain mists the black, gigantic vultures of Bombay. Yet, withal, the dog teams hurried by, their nostrils lengthened with the congealing air, their mouths firmly closed as with a lock, while the driver ran behind the loaded sleigh; and as they passed I did not know whether they should be pitied or praised.

This is a fearful place for one to live in throughout his life, or even for a single winter. It is so cold, so cold, that energy, ambition, and even life itself, seem not worth the value of a warm fire and a comfortable apartment.

The day after (November 18) there came to us at Dawson the news of a dreadful death. No one seemed surprised, no one made many comments; it appeared so possible, so natural, so easy to believe, that we simply drew closer to the fire, and wondered where we should be next winter. A miner was walking up the Klondike ten miles from here going to his claim. The Klondike is fed by numerous soda springs rushing down the banks during the long, hot summer days. These are so potent that even the winter's cold fails to close them entirely. Apparently the soda or alkali in these springs resists the action of frost better than simple water; so, therefore, it often happens that, walking on the edge of the ice near the shore, the footsteps suddenly sink through the weakened ice and into the bubbling alkaline waters that have stealthily worked their way beneath to the deep-flowing stream at the bottom. It was only 6 inches of water that the miner stepped into, and in a moment he was out, and, hastening to the brush hard by, started to light a fire: for the clothes freeze, the feet freeze, and in five minutes one may find that part of his body and garments which has been immersed in the water, though only a few inches deep, as rigid as solid steel. Rapidly he cut a few fragments of wood with his heavy pocket-knife. But the unlighted match dropped from his already chilled fingers, for he had rashly removed his mitts in order to use the knife with more freedom. Then he lighted a second and a third, and finally several at one time; but either haste, or perhaps a sigh of the air, caused them to fall on the ever-ready snow. And all this time the frost was seizing his limbs, his body, his heart, his mind. He turned to the fatal mitts, which he never should have taken off; but his already frozen fingers could only lift them from the ice where they had fallen, and after a vain attempt he hurled them from him, and strove once again to light a last match. But it was too late. Though only five minutes could have gone by, the terror of death was upon him. The Ice King slew him with appalling rapidity, and when his companion arrived, scarce fifteen minutes later, he found the body already cold and rigid, kneeling on the snow and ice, while the hands, partially closed together and uplifted as if in adoration or prayer to God, held yet within their palms the unlighted match. They said particles of the ice-laden air, minute and invisible, floated down to his lungs and killed him as would prussic acid. It was found impossible to remove his arms and hands from the attitude of entreaty in which they were placed, and the body was brought so to Dawson, and later buried without attempting to change their position.

On December 21 the sun rose at ten and set at two; thermometer 45° below zero. Withal, the stars were so bright, and the ice and snow so clear in the transparent atmosphere, that it was quite as easy to travel by night as by day.

On Christmas night a party of us dined at the principal restaurant. The dinner included moose, caribou, and ptarmigan. The moose and caribou were killed up the Klondike, east of Dawson, in the recesses of the Rocky Mountains, where large herds roamed. The hunters sledded the meat on dog-sleds down the Klondike, and sold it in Dawson at half a dollar per pound – the same price as frozen beef. The game meat was hard and close, and did not taste so well as the frozen beef from the "outside," which seemed far the better. It was odd to walk round Dawson and see carcasses of moose and caribou hanging side by side with carcasses of sheep and cattle. The price was uniformly the same. Ptarmigan, lovely in their snowy plumage, were shot even in the environs of Dawson, and especially up the Klondike. They made a delicious roast with dressing, and were numerous.

Hares and mountain sheep could also be procured at the butchers' shops. The former were large and the latter magnificent creatures, with thick curved, spiral horns. One could believe the tales the hunters told of these sheep pitching headlong 50 feet down a glacier, when pursued, and dropping on their horns, that penetrated the hard blue glacier ice, but yet did not break.

All of the wild animals, even to the little gophers, which run swiftly over the snow, living Heaven knows how, were clothed in spotless purest white. It was their winter garment of repentance. Occasionally we had grayling from the lakes, caught through holes in the ice. The grayling is about 9 inches long, one of them making a good meal, and found in all the lakes and in the Upper Yukon. These cold waters cause the fish to be firm and hard, and it is a delightful dish all the year round. We had frozen oysters in tins, and all kinds of canned meat and vegetables. But the moose and other game gave us ample supplies, and the canned meats went a-begging, though at gradually reduced figures.

One could feel that the country was changing, and that the ensuing year would bring more and varied comforts of a more permanent character.

Chapter 7

THE FIRST SLEIGH JOURNEY

On January 11, 1899, we started on a dog-sleigh journey through the mining districts. The party included Morton, Harry Munn, myself, and five dogs driven tandem. Harry Munn was a typical Klondiker. He had graduated, I believe, at Cambridge, and with honours. I first met him at St. Michaels, in July, 1898. He had followed the ice from the lakes down the Yukon for 1,800 miles in a Peterborough canoe, equipped with a sack of flour, a frying-pan, and a shotgun.

Ducks and geese were almost as numerous as mosquitoes. In the late evenings – for it was not sunset until eleven – he would steer to a sandspit, gather some of the always plentiful brush, light a fire, and on a pointed stick fry one of the tender ducklings or goslings shot during the day. Thereafter he would get afloat again, and coil comfortably in the middle of the boat while it glided peacefully down the calm though rapid current. There were no shoals nor cataracts, and if the Peterborough ran ashore either on a sandy island or the mainland, why, the jar awoke him, and, pushing the canoe off into deep water, he settled for another nap.

Harry had come back to Dawson, and now, having returned again from a caribou hunt on the head waters of the Klondike, he gladly joined us for this trip. He was our charioteer. The dogs, of whom three were Malamutes and two from the "outside," were not supposed to be of the very best quality. A fine team of young Malamutes had, indeed, been engaged for us by Harry; but the day before a stampede occurred, and their owner let them for more money to some stampeders.

We could complain, and perhaps go to law, but what was the use? Only a verbal agreement had been made, and no money paid over. Besides, business affairs were a little loose that winter in Dawson. People were only just becoming acquainted, and a feeling existed that, if one made a mistake; he was perhaps justified in receding if not too late. So, after making sundry and various remarks, we commissioned Harry to pick up what he could from the dregs of the dog-market, and left at the appointed hour. Morton, who made the third in our company, was going over the creeks, and on his return to Dawson would report his observations and conclusions to his principals in London.

It was cold, crisp, and clear as a desert atmosphere, when we dashed through the long, silent street on the Yukon bank. The river surface was smooth as marble, not a line disturbing the snow covering except the slender trail to White Horse, and the still more slender trail straight across to West Dawson. Though the doors of all the cabins were closed, and masses of ice were packed like logs on the sills and sides, the smoke came comfortably out of the chimney-tops, and the people we met, though clad like Eskimos, yet looked ruddy and cheerful as they shouted "Good-bye!"

From the end of the street we tumbled over the bank on to the Klondike, and took the trail midway on its icy covering for Hunker Creek. Directly after leaving the junction of the Yukon and the Klondike, we saw on our right numerous cabins. No smoke issued from any of them, yet they lined the bank for a mile or two. They were relics of the "'97 Stampede."

People had to live somewhere and so built these little homes, only to leave them, after the winter, silent and desolate. There seems to be nothing permanent in this country, unless it is the handiwork of God.

After leaving this hamlet of deserted cabins, we passed the mouth of Bonanza Creek, and continued our journey, noting many small birch-trees on the hill-slopes that bounded both banks of the Klondike.

The sleigh sped after the galloping dogs with scarce a sound. Harry stood erect behind on the rudder. The team needed no guide, for the trail was narrow, clear, and walled with snow-banks. Presently, in spite of the wolf, dog, and lynx robes enveloping us, I began to feel a deadly cold slowly paralysing my feet and hands.

"Harry," I said, "I can't stand this; I am freezing. We'll have to stop and light a fire."

"Nonsense," said this veteran of one Arctic winter. "I'll get you warm." He opened the robes in which, enveloped like a mummy, I reclined on the sleigh, and giving me a smart push, rolled me out of the sled, which was only a foot high, into the soft snow that bordered the ice. "Now," he shouted, "pick yourself up and come on."

I jumped to my feet to see the tail of the sleigh just disappearing round a curve. It was no time for remonstrances – besides, there was no one to listen; and so, without any delay, I started to leg it for all I was worth. It surprised me to note how fast I could run, and with how little fatigue. I wore felt shoes, and my robes were on the sled. I must have run near a mile, with stoppages for rest, when finally

Harry, who had tantalizingly kept ahead just out of reach, arrested the panting dogs, who at once curled up just where they stopped. That was their manner of resting.

I was not overfatigued nor overheated, so intense was the cold and so necessary are physical movements to combat its force. Shortly after we started I had the pleasure of tumbling Morton overboard, when he least expected it, to my great gratification. He was short and corpulent, and it was with infinite pleasure that I contemplated the beads on his balmy brow when Munn, in response to his piteous appeals for mercy, let him approach after half an hour's running. We did this same thing again, nevertheless, at intervals during the day. It was absolutely necessary for our preservation. Munn, the marvelous, ran like an Indian for half the distance, sometimes ahead, encouraging the dogs to come on, then at the sides, and finally, with one foot on a board projecting behind, he stood upright like a vertical rudder, directing the movements of the dogs with his voice and a long whip. "Gee," "Ha," and "Mush," comprise the full extent of a good driver's vocabulary, with perhaps a few minor words as adjuncts. "Gee" means to the right; "Ha," to the left; and "Mush," go on. The latter is a corruption of the French *marchons*, and indicates how the French-Canadian voyageurs have implanted their language on the habits as well as the place-names of the new North-West.

We passed numerous pedestrians going to and from Dawson. Those returning up the creeks were loaded to the hips. It is astonishing how great a weight on the back and shoulders a man can sustain and walk with ease. I can well believe that the average equipment of a Roman soldier weighed 60 pounds, when we met stalwart miners plodding sturdily along in this bleak atmosphere, carrying on their broad backs, on a pack-saddle especially contrived for men, flour, bacon, and other food-supplies, with an axe, a stove, and in some instances a tent. These men were too poor not only to keep a dog, but even to buy a hand-sleigh that might cost 20 dollars. But they were surcharged with hope, good health, and cheerfulness. Not one was despondent or lachrymose. The brilliant, pellucid, sparkling atmosphere exalted the mind while it fortified the body. They stepped jauntily along, and always had the last word as we cantered past them.

"Hello, pard!" Harry said to one as we came up; "you look tired."

"Not a bit," he replied; "but your cheeks are as white as a little girl's. Better get down and rub them."

That meant frost, and the admonition was not unheeded.

"Where will you camp to-night?"

"Oh, don't know; first road-house, I guess, if they don't take all we have."

"Where are you going?"

"Upper Hunker."

"Want a lift for a couple of miles?"

"No, guess not. Would freeze up in your darned old sleigh; this is all right."

And we left him trudging bravely along. There is, however, a certain privation for the traveller during the Arctic day. He cannot either drink or smoke while travelling: if he smokes, his breath drops frozen to the ground – that is, all that does not remain in icicles around his beard or mouth, like the facial ornaments of Santa Claus; if he drinks, the sudden warming of the stomach by the liquor is succeeded by an equally sudden cooling, and the reaction is unpleasant, if not dangerous. But still one has the evening and night for compensation.

We galloped twenty-five miles, and stopped for the night at Roadhouse 54 below on Hunker; that is to say, at the fifty-fourth claim below "Discovery" – i.e., the first claim staked out on Hunker Creek. It was a large cabin consisting of one immense room containing three stoves, with spruce beams spanning the roof arch, 45 feet from end to end. There were twenty-four empty bunks, built like the steerage accommodation on an Atlantic liner. Every traveller carried his own robes and blankets. The only woman cooked a good meal of caribou, evaporated potatoes, and canned salmon, but no sugar, for the twelve or fifteen wayfarers who had gathered for the night. Her husband was busy splitting logs of wood to a size suitable for the two other large Yukon stoves, and keeping them filled. Despite this superabundance of fuel, the wooden walls of the cabin were inlaid with white hoar-frost, though the ceilings were clear. The place was lighted by two large oil-lamps hanging irregularly from the wall, which gave not enough brightness even to read. After supper we all crouched round the biggest stove, and talked of what the weather would be to-morrow, and of mining prospects. There were no chairs, and only two small dubious benches. I observed that no one either told where he came from or asked others. The "outside" was an interdicted subject. Indeed, we did not discuss the bits of news that the Dawson papers had gleaned from occasional papers or travellers that had lately arrived. One might have been a prince or a peasant in the "outside"; here in the "inside" we were all equal.

At ten o'clock the husband and wife retired to two adjacent bunks, and we followed their example. Though the husband rose several times to replenish the fire in the big stove, yet I suffered severely from the cold, even under my lynx robe. One might almost as well have been in the open air, the log hut was so vast and gloomy.

The next morning Harry called us betimes, but we were not ready. We were sore and cramped in our legs and feet after yesterday's running.

"Go and feed the dogs," I said, "and come back."

"I fed them last night."

"Yes, but what has that to do with this morning?"

"Only that they are never fed but once in twenty-four hours when travelling."

I was amazed.

"Is that so?"

"Yes, and they thrive under it. Don't you remember how fast we made the last couple of miles yesterday?"

"Yes; what then?"

"Well, the dogs saw the road-house in the distance, and knew a hot supper was waiting for them as well as ourselves."

How different from horses, which require to be fed so frequently!

At eleven we started, with inward and outward groans and trepidations. But our legs braced up, and under the sharpened spur of the calm cold we ran briskly. In a couple of hours we made a cabin, and were given a good hot dish of beans and bacon. Our host was a man whom his miners called "Judge." And, with his kindly and cordial greeting, he seemed a judge of courtesy and good taste. Doubtless he had earned the title justly in other lands. We did not even ask his name. Those little things do not seem to signify.

On we went, the dogs labouring heavily through loose snow that had gathered upon the usually clear ice trail. Our traps weighed 250 pounds, and that, with the heavy sleigh, made hard pulling. Morton and myself had to walk or run the whole distance. When the sled stuck and Harry called on the dogs, they would, with wild barks, jump into the air, spring forward, and almost break the slender traces in frantic efforts to start. The Malamutes especially, if these efforts were not successful, bent themselves until they looked like snakes, forced their paws through the snow to the hard ice beneath, and pulled like tigers. All this with only vocal encouragement and not a touch of the long, light whip-lash. One would not have expected such eager devotion and fierce determination from partially wild dogs. The quarter-strain of wolf seems to have tempered the three-quarters of civilized blood, so that for strength and steadiness on a long journey they are more serviceable than giant Danes or Newfoundlands.

Finally we came to Discovery, where lived Andy Hunker, who first found gold thereon and gave his name to the creek. The road-house in the vicinity I found, to my surprise, was kept by a Swedish woman who, with her family of grown sons and daughters, had made with me the voyage from San Francisco to Dawson via St. Michaels. She had built the place on Discovery, by the grace of Andy, whom she subsequently married, and was doing a thriving business, for this part of the country was well filled with miners, and a number of claims were worked.

After supper we went over to Andy's snug and warm cabin. The hospitable old "sourdough" – i.e., old-timer – greeted us with a broad smile and with Scotch and water.

"Well," he said, in answer to our queries, "I've been here since September 18, 1896, when I first found gold. I left Forty Mile directly after we heard that Carmack had discovered gold on Bonanza; but before I arrived every spot on Bonanza that looked good was taken up. I was too slow. You see," he continued with a sigh, "I've been in this country on and off a dozen years, and I don't move round as spry as I used to once. But it's all right now," he added, taking a drink of Scotch straight that would have floored most men, and wiping his mouth with the back of a hairy hand. "It's all right, and I don't mind. After I found I was too late for Bonanza and Eldorado, I wandered over this way, crossing the mountains and hunting moose. When I came to this creek I thought it looked likely for gold, and I prospected with pan and shovel for a fortnight. At last I struck it pretty good, and went down to Forty Mile to locate. Then I started back with some grub for winter, with Johnson here to help me." He pointed to a stolid Swede of giant bulk and Viking hair, who filled the cabin. "We had to come up on the west side of the Yukon, because the ice was too thick on this side. It was hard, very hard, work, pulling the boat against the water, for ice was forming everywhere, and, you see, we had no time to lose. Often we went into the water to our hips, and we didn't have no rubber boots. The water was cold, very cold," he added reflectively. "We towed when we couldn't do anything else. The small cottonwood-trees were that thick on the bank that we had to cut through them with an axe sometimes when towing, to make headway with the rope. Ah, that was a vera hard trip, vera hard trip for fourteen days! We had no tent, and slept in our blankets with the atmosphere below zero every night. We only slept four or five hours, and then went at it again; for if the ice froze around our boat we were gone, and the glass was dropping lower and lower each night. But we got here all right, built this nice cabin right away, and have stayed with it ever since."

Andy looked round complacently on the dirty floor, the two small bunks, the grimed window constructed of old ale-bottles, and the dark blackened rafters above.

On a small shelf were some books. I examined them. They included six volumes of Gibbon.

"Who left these here?" said I to Andy.

"Who left them here?" he answered sharply; "why, no one. I've had 'em for two or three years. Take 'em everywhere, and read 'em nearly every night when I get time. I'll bet I know more about Caesar, Hadrian, Attila, Belisarius, and all the others, than you do – or most anyone else," he continued triumphantly.

I looked at the covers and leaves, dirty but not dusty, and then, with respect, on the sturdy old man who preserved so unique a taste in such a place and with such surroundings.

In the morning Andy took us over his claims, and gathered a pan of dirt scraped from the bottom of a ten-foot shaft. The pan was washed in a big tub filled with water obtained by boiling ice continually in a pot on the stove. When the pan was emptied of gravel, stones, and dirt, there remained about 5 dollars' worth of coarse gold – lumps, that is, averaging from 10 cents to 50 cents. They looked shining and attractive, despite the cold and bleak surroundings, and I breathed an inward prayer that I might have something of the same kind before long. Hunker thinks there is 1,000,000 dollars gross in his ground. I hope there is, for it will be beneficial to all the Klondike.

After paying 18 dollars in dust for our night's lodging, sleeping in our own robes, and having for food poor beans, bacon, coffee, and bread, we left about eleven. Up from the narrowing valley rose spirally clouds of white smoke, obscuring and perceptibly warming the air. These clouds came from the burning wood used for thawing.

Every half-mile we met a group of heavily-clothed men working round a shaft. The shafts were 6 feet in diameter, and seldom timbered. Wood – mostly birch, for that lasts longer – was placed in the bottom of the shaft, loose dirt thrown on top, and then the wood was lighted. It burned and smouldered ten hours before being entirely destroyed. This process warmed the gravel below to a depth of 2 feet, which was at once taken out by the miners and the process renewed.

The dirt was removed by means of a windlass and oddly-shaped bucket, the latter holding 150 pounds; one man below to pick and shovel in, and one at the windlass. It seemed pitiful to see a man standing on the frail platform, slowly turning the tedious windlass in a keen, biting atmosphere 45° below zero. Indeed, as I often thought, these men who come here and work thus deserve all they find, and more. One man we watched for a while with curiosity and sympathy. He was working entirely alone. Down a slender ladder he would descend twenty-five steps to the bottom. Filling the bucket, he would then ascend the ladder, windlass the bucket up wearily and painfully, and then down again to repeat the process, like the toils of Sisyphus. He did not stop to speak or rest as we looked on, but silently and steadily continued his labours.

We were told later that he was a carpenter from St. Louis, who had a 2,000 dollar mortgage on his home there, where lived his wife and young children. If not paid in the spring the mortgage would be foreclosed. Hence his fierce, tireless efforts to extract the gravel for the spring wash-up. No one would work for or with him, for it was doubted if that ground contained much gold. We went on with a silent wish and hope for his success. I never heard of him afterwards, nor of his success or failure, although I made inquiries. People disappear in this country like a pebble in the water, and with equal suddenness.

Later in the afternoon we came to the steep pass that divides Hunker from Dominion. I challenged Morton to walk straight up the deserted tramway ascent leading directly to the summit, 1,000 feet above. He is short, stout, stumpy, and over 15 stone, but without a word – for he had no breath to spare – dropping his heavy wolf-skin robe on the sleigh, he dared the icy chute. Formerly a windlass at the top with rope attachment, and ties like railway ties laid crossways every 6 feet, made the ascent comparatively easy. However, a free trail constructed by the Government, less steep, made the private tramway unnecessary, and it was abandoned. Up we clambered, mostly on our hands and knees. Strangely enough, Morton led me by quite a distance. Then he stopped to breathe, and while looking in triumph down on my twisting form crawling carefully up a few feet below, and digging my heels into the ice banked against the ties, he said: "This is nearly –" Thus far had he spoken, and no further, when – something gave way and down he went tobogganing by me like a motor-car. I waited until he brought up in a bank of snow 50 feet below, and then remarked distinctly and pleasantly:

"I suppose you were going to say 'This is nearly hell – or heaven' – which was it?"

What breath was left in him couldn't speak, and looks don't kill at 50 feet, so I left him to his reflections and toiled my way to the top, where he joined me a few minutes later. Forty degrees below zero, clear, a piercing cold, yet we threw ourselves down exhausted on the snow that crowned the summit, with moisture on our brows and panting hurriedly.

A hundred miles away to the east the Rocky Mountains lifted their lofty glacial tops, kissing the blue, clear sky that bent to meet them, whilst nearer rose lower ranges, making clear the lines of the Klondike, and even of the Yukon. Far up to the northeast could be seen lancet-shaped hills, whence issued the first waters of the Klondike, and where roamed the moose, caribou, and mountain-sheep. Nearer, the hills bent lower to the valleys, and forests were visible, while to the west and north again loomed vast mountains, bleak, desolate, arid, and icy. Oh, but it made one shiver even to look on the whiteness and blankness of an Arctic winter scene.

Around a curve in the Government road just below us appeared Harry, loaded up till he resembled a moose. He staggered up and fell breathless, letting fall a mass of robes.

"What's the matter? Where's the dogs?" we demanded, and visions of accidents, falling over precipices, with the nearest road-house twenty miles away, came to our minds.

"Nothing – Government road," he gasped. "Why, the dogs can't pull the empty sled up this damned road, let alone anything in it. I've left them half dead a couple of hundred yards below, and I must go back for another load."

Of such hardy and determined men are made the pioneers of empires.

We looked at him, the robes and the road. The latter seemed steep and precipitous enough to tax one's energies in climbing its slippery acclivities, without an ounce more to carry. But Morton said cheerily – we were getting cold by now:

"Well, we'll go down and give you a lift."

And his rotund, robust shape rolled adown the pass like a short ship in a sharp gale.

We followed and found the dogs, with the remaining robes and eatables, all piled high on the sled, itself lost in a snow-bank 10 feet deep. Evidently the dogs had tried to follow their master, with this exasperating result. It was no time to wonder or explain. We cut the dogs' traces, threw the load off the sleigh, and with great exertion got it back to the road again. Morton harnessed the dogs and went ahead, while Harry and myself staggered up the trail with what odds and ends were left. That was a bad quarter of an hour. The sun's rays, as frequently happens even in this midwinter, had softened the surface of the ice, and the steel runners, instead of gliding over, had sunk through the surface for an inch or two. When this occurred, the dogs, faithful brutes as they were, absolutely could not move the light though long sleigh without assistance. We threw down our loads, pushed and pulled, dogs and men all together, until we got on a bit, and then went back and carried up our things. We had plenty of whisky, but dared not touch a drop.

At length we reached the point which Morton and myself had surmounted two hours before. If the Government official who surveyed that "trail" had been present then – well, he would certainly have been made to bear his share of the burdens, together with sundry criticisms.

However, we had to get on without delay. Everything, including Morton and myself, was piled in pell-mell, and Harry Munn started the dogs at a fearful rate down the pass, which was just as steeply inclined as on the side we had just left. Harry stood on the rudder behind, erect as the long spar of a racing yacht, yelling with fiendish energy to the dogs. These latter had to keep on. If one stumbled or fell, it made no difference. They were all attached to a light line, and if one did not keep his feet he was simply dragged along with the procession until he found them again. My heart was in my mouth, and I clung desperately to the sled when we whirled down and round the sharp curves, sending splinters of ice and showers of snow into the air like a cloud. Like Mary's little lamb, I was resolved that wherever the sled went I would go, too.

It was all right so long as the leader kept his feet. He was an intelligent little dog of the Scotch collie type, and led the rush swiftly down the steep slopes, the Malamutes baying like hounds. But five dogs tandem, followed by an eight-foot sled, even if it is but 18 inches wide, make a snaky string to guide, and so it happened that the rear end of the off steel runner struck a tough bit of ice that lay on the trail. *Kerchunk!* and the sled went off into the air like a balloon, then down the mountain-side amid the snow, carrying with it the howling dogs, who in this case followed instead of preceding. Presently Harry, who had stepped off a story or two above when we left the road, rolled down to where Morton and myself were contemplating the disorder from under our bed-quilts of snow, and said pleasantly:

"How are you? Don't you think it's time to be up and moving? We can't stay here all night, you know."

Oh, he was very calm and consoling, was that same Harry Munn!

"Get the dogs and the sleigh and the whisky and things and the snow off us, and we will certainly arise," said I.

He did so, and we then arose. It was not so bad, after all. Nothing was broken, and one does not get a bruised body in a snowdrift. To be sure, it was hard for our tired limbs to put the whole outfit back on the trail again. Even the very dogs had to be assisted through the deep, soft snow to the road above. But it was a down grade when we started off, and that made it easy.

At seven o'clock in a starlit night, with the Aurora spanning the heavens like a bracelet of brilliant diamonds, we dashed up to No. 11 below Discovery on Dominion Creek, owned by a French-Canadian. A good warm meal of Klondike strawberries [beans], with bacon, bread, and evaporated potato accompaniments, and we sought repose. The bedchamber was an adjunct to the bar and dining-room, there being actually two rooms in the cabin. We found no bunks, but a platform about a foot from the floor extending to the wall. Side by side lay six sleeping men, while a glimmering stove out of the darkness gave forth an uncertain light and heat. We soon made the six nine, lying by each other like logs, but sleeping soundly and tranquilly.

The next two days were taken up with visiting and examining a few of the mines. The method of working I found to be about the same in all: sinking by burning wood down to bedrock – that is, 20 or 30 feet – and then running tunnels in various directions along this rocky floor, whereon lies most of the gold. Between the tunnels cross ones were dug, and the dirt to a height of 8 feet broken

down and taken to the surface, there to lie until
spring when water came. We found in one or tw
decidedly primitive manner of sinking a shaft.
merely this: Flat, circular stones, 2 feet in diametei ...nd 6
inches thick, were heated in a wood fire on the surface for a
couple of hours; they were then placed side by side in the
bottom of the shaft. It is claimed that these hot stones
soften and thaw the frozen gravel deeper and quicker than a
wood fire, and that it takes less wood thoroughly to heat the
stones than to thaw the ground direct by burning. I doubt
this, however, as I saw very few using this method, which
might be termed primitive and experimental. Trees of any
kind and size are scarce on Dominion Creek, and the fuel
question is important.

Though several hundred men were working patiently,
yet the results did not seem to us very fruitful. The shafts
were deeper, more water was found on bedrock, and the
pannings appeared to be poorer than on Bonanza or Eldorado. Moreover, the valley of the creek was over half a
mile wide in places, and I had already learned that the
wider the pay streak, the less the concentration of gold, and
naturally the higher the cost of production.

While visiting the different mines, the dogs fairly
leaped over the snow. The weather was pronounced perfect, only 20° below zero; the sun shining brightly; the tops
of the low hills crowned by small birch-trees, with
branches glistening like pearls in the sunlight. Everyone,
including even the toiling dogs, was happy and cheerful.

For dinner we had moose meat. It was fresh, and therefore tough, but it was the first I ever ate, and I could not get
enough. We had taken a few bottles of California claret
with us, being a remnant of two small barrels that I had

brought from San Francisco, and we felt like Roman banqueters. The road-house owner was a French-Canadian, whose words were difficult to understand. His French might have been pure in the days of Louis XIV, but it certainly would not be comprehended on the boulevards today. Yet it is astonishing and admirable that his race should so tenaciously have retained their ancient language, far distant and isolated from France as they have been these two or three centuries.

I understood Cachenard's English but little better than his French, for all that he and his ancestors for generations were Canadians. They are not very learned, these voyageurs, and the healthful life of the woods, lakes, and rivers of the North-West seems to have fully satisfied their mental as well as physical wants.

Chapter 8

ELDORADO AND BONANZA

Early on the 16th we left Dominion for Sulphur Creek by way of Caribou. The trail, though difficult, was yet a gradual ascent until we came to near the top. There we found it much sharper, and had to make two trips to get all our belongings on to the summit. We met quite a number of men with sleds and dogs, and passed two travellers walking together, each of them carrying on his sturdy back over a hundredweight of provisions and mining tools. How they ever went up that divide, and especially the last bit, where it was steep enough to make a hard climb without any burden, I cannot imagine. The poor devils were evidently on a prospecting expedition, and had only money to purchase a little food for themselves.

The valley of Dominion Creek, which we had just left, lay far below, like a large basin, encompassed by snowy mountains. Here and there it was sparsely covered with trees, and the occasional spirals of thin white smoke rose up like genii into the clear, crisp atmosphere. A mile or two on the level summit, with its white, snowy shroud, and, lo! a roadhouse. But, alas! when Harry asked the owner, "When can we have something to eat?" he sharply replied:

"Ain't got nothing. The stampeders took all our grub."

"What! Stampeders!" said I.

"Wall, don't you know there's a stampede on to Gold Run? They've been passing here since nigh on to two o'clock this morning. All grub gone, and only one bottle whisky left," he added with a contented air.

This stampede business, then, that I had heard of so often, was really true. We learned from the proprietor of the road-house, who, being two-thirds drunk, was half sulky – though he should have been well satisfied to have disposed of his stuff at ounce figures – the following facts:

Two Canayens had sleighed into Dawson the day before from Gold Run, forty miles away. They had exhibited gold-dust, made proper affidavits, received Governmental acknowledgments of their locations from the Land Office, and, after buying supplies, immediately departed. It was an obscure creek, dismal and distant, but yet – for some officials are leaky casks – the rumour was bruited. One told another; he whispered to a third; this to a fourth; and presently the stampede commenced. On foot, with dogs of varying sizes and breeds, with and without food for dog or man, they rushed out into the cold, piercing frost, eager to climb the ice, snow, mountains and glaciers that fronted them, for the Golconda forty miles distant. So it happened that, as many came this particular route, the road-house people had disposed of their limited supply. There was nothing else to do but, metaphorically, buckle our belts and continue the journey.

The summit was a terrace eight miles long and a mile wide, quite level, and covered with 5 feet of snow, smooth as alabaster. The trail, a couple of yards wide, lay between the lines of snow, worn down to the hard, blue ice, the contrast reminding one of a bunch of dark violets lying between two banks of white carnations. A tiny gopher ran across the trail, his white fur glistening as he barely escaped the eager fangs of the hungry leader. How they live in and under this snow during the dreary winter months I do not know. I suppose some sustenance must be found on the frozen ground. He was quite small, little larger than a mouse, and was doubtless not alone. It would seem that no place on earth is so completely desolate that no animal life exists. Very likely, when the North Pole is reached, it will be found covered by a herd of musk-oxen.

An hour's canter of dogs and men, and we came to the descent leading down to Brimstone Creek. The outlook filled us with dismay. Our sleigh was 8 feet by 18 inches. With the five dogs in line, the stretch from rudder to leader's nose was quite 25 feet; but below us the trail seemed to be no longer than 5 feet. At least, it disappeared every 5 feet amid the trees, which made a thick forest, to reappear again below.

Harry was captain of the ship when voyaging. He promptly made his decision and issued his orders.

"The whole thing can't go together, as the trail is too narrow and crooked. The dogs must be unhitched and taken to the bottom of the pass. I'll run the sled down myself."

Morton, who, unlike most Scotsmen, was always looking for an easy task, at once volunteered to pilot the dogs. We knew well that they would pilot him. The traces were unhitched from the sled, leaving the dogs still fastened together. Off they started, barking and leaping high into the air, in the freedom of restraint from the heavy sleigh, with Morton falling and floundering along, but holding the reins well, and checking the headlong dash as best he could. After they had whirled down out of view, I seemed to have no use for myself.

"What will I do, Harry?" I asked, anxious to be of some good.

"Nothing. Get down to Brimstone without breaking your neck. I'll do the rest."

"Nonsense," I said cheerily; "I will help you with the sled."

"What can you do?" he said, with an odd smile.

"Why, I'll stand on the rudder and help turn around the corners."

"Oh, that's all right. Get on;" and away we were, he running ahead of the sled with a light line in his hand, as active as a leopard.

We two – that is, the sled and I – followed like an elephant or hippopotamus, until, alas! at the turning, a birch-tree barred our way like a stone wall. The sled stopped. I didn't, but kept on. I avoided the tree, but buried myself in a snow-bank so deep that I was physically inconspicuous. Mr. Harry Munn calmly waited while I sputtered up. He never offered to help me.

"Have to hold the sled, you know."

"Why, I think the tree is doing that very well," I replied indignantly.

But he continued: "How do you like your new job? I didn't ask you to help me, you know."

This was gratitude! And away up in the Arctic regions!

"I'll tell you," I humbly admitted, "I don't think I'm a success as an upright mast, but how would I serve as a horizontal rudder?"

"What's that?" he exclaimed.

I was anxious to do something to show my usefulness and inventive faculties in an emergency.

"I'll lie down on the back of the sled, with my legs behind, and when we come to a sharp turn I'll hold my legs stiff the other way, and down we'll go like a skid."

"Very well, we'll see," he replied grimly, and off he started, before I had fairly secured a position in which effectually to exercise my new functions.

All went well for awhile; but alas for the futility of men's best wishes! The tree we had first encountered was not, I ascertained, the only one on the mountain; in fact, there were thousands of them, and it was unfair and unreasonable not to greet at least a few more. On this occasion, however, I found the position of my rudder legs prevented me from going ahead, but not aside, and as the sled attempted to climb the tree on one part, I just toppled over the bank on the other. It became inspiriting. I rose like Antæus, shook my body free from the entwining snow-wreaths, and mounted once again, regardless of sundry sarcastic observations by good, gentle Harry Munn. In time we came to the bottom. Toward the last Harry had to run behind, and not in advance, for the sled, when the pass was fairly straight, flew on like a leaf. At the end we came upon Morton calmly smoking the pipe of peace, with the dogs, like children, curled around him.

"Well, well!" he said, when I told him of my perils, struggles, and adventures.

And that was all, but he continued smoking while we fastened dogs and vehicle together. My phlegmatic Scotsman!

Along the level we dashed, passing a few cabins with their white smoke glimmering under the stars of the night, and at six of the evening we doubled up in front of road-house Brimstone, after which the creek is named. The cabin of Brimstone is at 7 Sulphur, the point where the Brimstone water joins with the latter creek. We were not specially fatigued, despite the long weary day and my various contusions. This marvelous climate develops the most superb physical energy and endurance. But we were hungry – oh, so hungry! We had had no lunch, be it remembered, for everything was eaten up at the Summit roadhouse. Brimstone was about the roughest place we had seen. No fresh meat or game, which hitherto we had eaten every night. The place was close and stifling, with two dreary candles dimly burning, and a dozen men crowded together in the only room. Most of them were smoking in the already dense atmosphere. A few dogs lay anywhere they could find room to curl up upon the floor. Miners' picks, shovels, blankets, with sacks of flour and flitches of bacon, were scattered anywhere, everywhere. It was like an old curiosity-shop. Yet we had a most excellent supper of canned pigs' feet and canned corn, with coffee. One can eat anything here with relish after travelling all day in the sharp, stinging air.

The glass outside marked 40° below. When the door opened, a white, blinding mist rushed in, filling the place instantly, and in the faint candlelight made us appear like ghostly figures. All the men were employed on Brimstone, except two or three prospectors. There was little conversation, and less jollity. They seemed morose and morbid. Packing men together like cattle causes irritability rather than good-fellowship. In the middle of the room was a large rudely-constructed box, filled with frozen dirt from the mine. This dirt was the day's samples, and in the morning, after thawing all night, it would be panned out, and the gold left would show the result. Around it, upon the cold

floor, several men lay on robes and blankets. The two small
stoves gave little heat against the fierce cold. Someone
seemed to be going out or coming in continually, and the
cabin appeared to be built of logs, without much moss or
mortar between them.

We slept two in a bunk. My comrade, close in against
the frosty wall, was a miner. He read a book by the light of
a bit of candle until midnight, and was extremely careful
not to disturb the sleepers. In the morning at six he arose.
Like the rest, he did not have to dress himself, but swung
down from his bunk even before the fires were lighted, and
read until breakfast. I tried to see the work in which he was
so much interested, but he carried it away.

The air was still quiet and clear on the upper reaches of
Sulphur, as we started homeward the next day. Small glaciers confronted us occasionally as we went higher up the
glen. Some of these, we were told, lasted throughout the
entire summer. There were birch, fir, and cedar forests on
the slopes and mountains above. We passed many cabins
and "dumps," most of the latter moderate in size.

Sulphur does not bear a good reputation. It is said to be
one of the poorest creeks in the Klondike, and certainly the
small "dumps" do not look cheering. But with all our trials
and travels, we were neither depressed nor fatigued.

At noon eight of us lunched in a little cabin 8 feet
square, and only the empty dishes were visible when we
stopped eating. Going up the mountain from the head of
Sulphur, though fatiguing, was not so difficult as other
parts of our journey had been, for the ascent was more
gradual. It makes all the difference in the world to dogs if
they can pull the sled steadily, without having to jump and
leap every few minutes to make headway.

This summit was bare of trees. A slight breeze blew over the snow, but not strongly enough to cause apprehension. I have never felt a really strong wind since I came to the Klondike. Indeed, people could not exist here in winter if there were blizzards. The Summit road-house contained three small rooms with a stove in each, but only the smallest was lighted. Wood was 95 dollars a cord, they told us. It was cold and cheerless, but our appetites, which were perennial, made up for other deficiencies.

Late at night two men entered, who sat by the stove and called for some food. One of them seemed slender and silent. He never spoke even to his companion, and sat in his fur cloak with his head down and averted. Very soon they went into the room where we all bunked together, and took one of the bunks. Morton turned to me, and said:

"That's a woman."

"What! in men's clothes, coming in this time of the night," I said.

"Yes," said Johnson, the owner, "sure enough, that's a woman; and what's more, they've come from Dawson, forty miles, in two days, walking every step of the trail. The man seems to be too poor to get a couple of dogs for the girl."

"How do you know she is a girl?"

"Well, she is, and a pretty one, too, with long black hair. She never expected to find a dozen men here, and her trousers and exhausted condition made her almost faint with shame."

"Where are they going?" enquired Harry.

"I don't know," said Johnson. "He asked no questions, and paid his bill in dust from a very small poke. I suppose he is some prospector, and the girl, whoever she may be, could not travel in woman's clothes over the ice and snow. Oh! I've seen curious sights and heard strange stories since I've kept this road-house, now nigh on to two years," said Johnson sagely, clearing his pipe and putting some dry birch into the stove.

At ten, before sleeping, I went out for a moment. From the summit the Aurora was marvelously brilliant, and the stars shone like red diamonds – a slight breeze, and the glass 42° below. The couple had a bunk directly opposite our own. A slender light came from the stove outside in the other room. There was no door. The frost lined the wooden wall behind and above my head like white lace embroidery, and the dogs grumbled in their sleep as they lay around the fire dying in the stove.

In the morning the man and woman were gone. Her fear and shame had aroused him, and they went forth, walking under the Aurora and the red diamonds of the Northern sky at midnight. I never knew who they were, nor if they arrived at their destination or perished in the night.

We left early, after a very poor breakfast of thin bacon, weak coffee, and hard biscuits made without baking-powder. This was unusual, for the roadhouses give good food and generously. Johnson, or Johanssen, was a Swede, however, and they are disposed towards economy. Then, he had had a great run of prospectors; besides, the snow was so deep it was hard for the dogs to pull a heavy load up the grade. He kept two teams, each of six dogs, making trips every four days to and from Dawson, forty miles away: two days from Dawson, one day back, and one day to rest and for purchases in town. Each sleigh carried about 1,200 pounds; but going up the Dome the load was divided, two trips being made from the head of Carmack's Forks to the road-house, eight miles farther up the mountain. We found that the trail still ascended, and in an hour we came to the real summit, rising sharply in a peak and unfolding a most sublime spectacle.

This immense mountain, called not inappropriately the Dome, dominates the whole environment. It was so termed because its shape is like a dome, and it was indeed a Pantheon high up amid the stars. Except the peak in the centre, it sloped upward very gently like an artificial terrace, covered with 5 feet of the purest snow, whose iced surface sparkled in the meagre sunlight. At its base stretched away and beyond all the gold-bearing watercourses, the higher hills near the Dome gradually disappearing in the flat valley, far away indeed, but yet visible in the transparent air. Hunker, Quartz, Sulphur, Dominion, Bear, and Bonanza, all led away in sinuous outlines like immense cobras from every side, while Cold Run, and even vistas of Indian River, could be seen to the south-west.

To the east, 100 miles distant, the Rocky Mountains showed their white lines, and to the south-east the course of the Klondike could be easily followed through the unbroken ranges of parallel mountains manacling the river between them. It was an exhibition of Nature in her boldest, coldest, and completest isolation. One could be lost in these bleak ranges as easily as at sea, and perish in a night.

The Dome itself bore no trees; in fact, the snow seemed to be a white tomb, for nothing appeared above its serene surface.

At Carmack's, the head of Bonanza Creek, we lunched on doughnuts and coffee, all the road-house larder possessed. Down Bonanza we sledded in a murky atmosphere, for many mines were worked and cabins abounded. Quite a number of miners on foot, laden with heavy packs, were met on the way to the different creeks, for this was the main trail from Dawson.

After a long, tedious journey, we came to the Grand Forks, and put up at one of the two hotels, not roadhouses, which was something of a change, if not relief. The supper was plentiful and excellent. Our bed or bunk consisted of a dirty sheet spread over unplaned boards – only this, and nothing more. Each traveller was supposed to provide his own bed-linen. We slept badly, for reasons. All sorts of noises sifted up through the chinks in the board floor of the second storey where we lodged – singing, swearing, drinking, dancing. It was a dollar a dance and drink, with ladies provided by the management. The poor devils of miners, after working hard during the day, had the dust filched from them in the night by these sirens, who picked out the lucky or reckless with unerring instinct. My senses were gradually deadened by the lullaby of the flute, fiddle and accordion; and I dreamed of the silent snow on the Dome and the woman in trousers.

It was late the next day when we harnessed the dogs after breakfast and went up Eldorado. Every mine on the creek was opened, and immense dumps loomed up like pyramids, palisaded to the tops. Hundreds of men were working for a dollar an hour, and the life around and about was cheering and comfortable. We stopped at Billy Chappell's, No. 97, Eldorado. Scarce thirty years old, an Antinous in form and face, with cheeks like two roses, and the eyes of a gazelle, this young Swede was said to be one of the most capable mine-owners in the Klondike. His half-interest in No. 27 on Eldorado cost 600 dollars two years ago, the sum being lent by Alex Macdonald, his associate.

The property has yielded thus far about 1,000,000 dollars. I had met Billy in Dawson frequently, and of course he knew Harry and Morton. He took us round the claim and down the shallow shaft only 15 feet deep. At its base the ground was thawed.

"Would you like to see a good pan?" he said to us.

"Yes, even if you don't present it to us as a souvenir," I replied.

"Oh, that's another thing," he laughingly said; "but you will see what we can do."

The foreman scraped together with his hands enough to fill the pan fairly, the dirt and gravel weighing, say, 25 pounds. It was taken into the cabin, washed and weighed. The result was 240 dollars in coarse, dark nuggets, running from 1 dollar to 20 dollars in value. We were astonished and enchanted, realizing in some measure the wealth of this Eldorado Creek. Chappell telephoned down to Stanley and Worden, whom we had passed at 24 on the way up – they had telephones there even in these days.

Connection made: "Charley, is that you?"

"Well, I've washed out a pan for Morton and the Senator – 240 dollars. Bet you the pan you can't do as well!"

"Take the wager. When are they coming down?"

"After dinner, and I'm going with them."

"All right. We'll be ready for you."

So late in the afternoon, after inspecting a number of other mines, only by no means so rich, we brought up at Charley Worden's. All hands went out to see the pan filled from the bedrock, going down a short shaft as in Chappell's mine. Of course, this place had been thawed the night before, otherwise the frozen surface would have turned the strongest steeled pick in two minutes. The foreman, who knew the best places, carefully gathered the dirt in his hands until the pan was filled. We could see lumps of gold here and there, and thought it would surpass Chappell's, but it only weighed 224 dollars.

"Charley," said Billy, "just put that gold into a small poke and let me take it home," which Charley ruefully did. "Now," added Billy with calm complacency, "we will drink some of your twenty-dollar champagne. The man that loses has to put up everything."

Never a word said Charley. He seemed crushed, and meekly, from some hidden spot, produced several quarts of champagne, costing in Dawson 20 dollars for each bottle. After a bottle or two he remarked:

"The only way for me to get even is to have you all stop for supper, and we will have some music afterwards."

"Music!" I exclaimed; "I don't see a piano." "Piano!" said Chappell; "what do you take us for? Do you think we are women or professionals? Besides, there are only two pianos in the Klondike; one is in the Monte Carlo, and the other in Tom Chisholm's Aurora."

"But," added Charley, "we have a fiddle, guitar, and flute, and once in a while we go down to the Forks and give them a concert." At which all shouted.

The supper was excellent, embellished with Scotch and champagne and good cigars. The two Stanley boys and Worden drifted in here from Seattle in the Carmack days, and each located a claim – Nos. 25, 26, 27, Eldorado – 500 feet in length linear measure, and extending from side to side of the creek, no matter how broad or narrow might be the valley. This was the mining law. Each of these three claims would produce an independent fortune, with very little labour and expense, as the channel was narrow, thus concentrating the gold, and the bedrock was comparatively close to the surface, 20 feet being a fair average.

Supper over, the neighbours dropped in, including three women, the only ones living in a radius of a couple of miles among 500 rough miners. An impromptu dance was organized on the rough floor after the table was removed. The two or three bunks in the corner and side made little difference. The orchestra, with Charley Worden as leader, stood where they could, while Scotch and champagne ad libitum were for all without stint. It must be remembered that Scotch whisky cost then 10 dollars a bottle, and it took no single nor light libation to satisfy these hardy men. But the "Eldorado kings" were generous in their warm hospitality. A rivalry between the leader of the orchestra and myself as to which played best or worst on the violin admitted of partisans to both sides. Harry said he liked the last of my playing the best, while Ned Stanley added that he liked his partner best when he didn't play at all. I don't know when or how the revelry ceased. I was oblivious in my bunk, from sleep or some other cause, and was laid there fully dressed. I knew Morton ought to be at my side, but when I awoke and arose in the early morn he was invisible. I felt his 220 pounds could not have entirely disappeared, and, not finding them among the sleepers scattered on the floor, wandered outside. A few feet from the cabin, lying in the deep snow by the trail, enveloped in his fur coat, he lay calmly sleeping, with his face exposed, and the temperature 25° below zero. I awoke him with difficulty.

"How in the wide world did you get out here?" I asked.

"I don't know very well," he answered when fully roused. "After everyone had gone home or to sleep in the cabin, I felt warm and came out."

"Do you know when that was?"

"Oh yes, at five o'clock. Let me see" – looking at his watch – "it's now seven. Why, I've only been here two hours. You might have left me alone a little while longer," he ruefully added, and went into the cabin grumbling, not in the least injured after sleeping for two hours with little protection in the snow and open air, under such intense cold that one could not expose the hand uncovered for three minutes without the fingers freezing. How considerate is Bacchus to his devotees!

We sent the dogs back to the Forks and footed it, thinking that better for our constitutions after the night's exertions. On the way we ascended French Hill, opposite 16. In August, when I was there, only two cabins occupied its surface. Now a little hamlet of more than fifty cabins existed, with others building. It was very rich in places, but the good ground seemed limited in extent. The air was not so muggy as the day before.

In August trees were very numerous; now they no longer existed. All had been cut down for fuel or timber. It seemed a desecration, yet this is essentially a mining country, and the wants of Nature must give way to the wants of man.

Descending into Eldorado, we continued down the creek, being much refreshed at the sight of the large workings exhibited on every side. That meant gold, and gold was what we all sought.

At Berry's No. 7 there was a two-storey house – not a cabin, but a good two-storey log house. Of course, that indicated women. Indeed, Mrs. Clarence Berry greeted us hospitably, and gave us fresh milk to drink. We, who had forgotten the taste of cream and milk, except in its condensed form, drank with thankfulness and amazement. It was even better than the best champagne at 20 dollars a quart. In a stable nearby she showed us, with pride, a genuine Jersey, wrapped in bandages like a mummy, but yet contentedly munching hay. The very stable was padded with sawdust – both walls, ceiling, and floor. The hay had been brought in from the "outside." The cow gave plenty of milk, so that, as Mrs. Berry said in triumph, "we have some of the comforts of civilization, no matter what they cost." Her husband was a Californian, who, with his brothers, had come among the first and fortunately staked on Eldorado; therefore they were independent, and could extract gold at leisure. I noticed as I left that the milk-bucket stood near the always heated stove.

It was late when we came to the Forks, and Gold Hill directly opposite was lighted up in the dusky gloaming like the night-fires on the walls of an embattled castle.

How did the gold find its way to the very summit of that hill instead of lying at its base, buried hundreds of feet under earth? Later I knew that this condition exists more or less over the entire country.

Our sleep was again invaded by the sounds from below. In addition, a party of drunken men and women occupied the adjoining compartment, separated only by a thin partition of lumber an inch thick, with plenty of crevices for sight-seeing as well as hearing. The charge is 2 dollars a meal and 2½ dollars for the privileges of a bunk. I shall avoid this place in the future. I much prefer the ordinary road-house, with its quiet, plain, homely, but comfortable and decent surroundings.

The next afternoon we left on foot for Dawson, fourteen miles. Harry Munn, with the dogs, had gone on to town. To try our condition after the eleven days' journey, the first either of us had made under similar conditions, and especially with such intense cold, we sprinted seven miles. It took us but an hour and a half, which was not bad walking. But it was a most beautiful road. The trail was wide, hard, and smooth. It was astonishing how much traffic and how many men, dogs, and horses, were going up and down between the Forks and Dawson. We were never alone the entire distance, and Bonanza Creek, down which we were walking, was a centre of activity in only less degree than Eldorado. On all sides were fires from shafts, cabins, and tents, while the air was thick with smoke. We met, among others, a couple of big horses pulling a large sleigh on which was loaded 3 tons of merchandise. That indicates how good a road it had become. We also met, to our surprise, many men living in tents. Two tents, one inside the other, with a space of 6 inches between filled partly, at least, with sawdust, made a haven nearly as warm and comfortable as a cabin, and very much cheaper. Every one had brought in some kind of a tent, while cabins had to be built, which meant time and money.

In the evening of that 22nd of January, 1899, we stalked into Dawson, proud of our prowess, 10 pounds lighter in the case of Morton, and correspondingly for myself, but feeling healthier, heartier, and happier, than at almost any other time in our lives. It is good to work, and it is better to finish with success. We knew now from our personal gleanings that this gold rush was not ephemeral, and would not end, as many feared, the following spring. We knew it would take years to exhaust the gravel beds, and that meant at least hope, if not success, for every one in the Klondike.

Chapter 9

THE STAMPEDE

It was eleven o'clock of a cold starry night. The Northern Lights "that came down o' nights to play with the houseless snow" flickered over the horizon, resplendent in their gray plumage. One could almost hear the rushing of giant wings sweeping the Ice King to the Pole.

But Dawson was strangely restless. Men glided round the street corners quietly and stealthily. Three met near the First Street Wharf.

"Where are the dogs?" said one.

"Here, below the bank on the river."

"Have you a tent?"

"No; we haven't time. I hear Jim Daugherty leaves at midnight."

"Where is he now?"

"In the Aurora; we have him under guard."

"Are many going?"

"I should think so. Billy Chappell, 'Skiff' Mitchell, and Charley Anderson go with Jim on his sled."

These were names to conjure with on the Klondike, for all three were successful miners.

"How many of the boys are on to it?"

"Holy smoke! I don't know, but dogs are everywhere. You can't turn a corner into any dark place without running into a team lying down on the snow."

"Are they taking much grub?"

"Some are taking a week's supply. Arnold says that Daugherty, when drunk last night, said he could get there in twenty-four hours if he wanted, but today they say he says it will take a week."

"Well, I'll go and get another side of bacon, and a small tent if possible. It's going to be devilish cold, and if there be any wind we'll have it rough, sure."

The speaker ran up toward the hill behind the town to his cabin, his moccasined feet touching the hard ice trail lightly and quietly. In the Aurora, standing at the bar amid a dense throng of curiously clad men, was Daugherty, taking his tenth Scotch-and-soda since dinner.

For several days it had been rumoured that he had made a new discovery. Certainly the presence of men like Chappell, Skiff, and Anderson, all of whom should have been out on the creeks, was suggestive. These miners were rich, and would not bother about an ordinary stampede. So it was that he had been shadowed, and the wise ones knew that the splendid team of eight Malamute dogs belonging to the Alaska Commercial Company had been harnessed to a sled loaded with supplies in the Company's yard since eight o'clock.

At midnight Jim drank a last glass with burly, good-natured Tom Chisholm, who wears a Panama hat all the winter, then slunk away toward the compound. Five minutes later his sled glided noiselessly to the smooth ice of the river trail. In with his three companions; a quiet, subdued, suppressed "Mush!" and the dogs sprang suddenly forward, their cushioned feet giving forth no sound, but leaping on like phantom wolves.

The steel-shod sled moved without noise. The men lay quiet, muffled in heavy robes, and the eight Malamutes, the 2,500 dollar prize team of the Klondike, sped down the river over the ice road, and vanished into the grayish, starlit mist that overhung the river, before the watchers had fairly recovered from their astonishment at the sudden, though anticipated, flight and disappearance.

But there were others on the alert also, and one by one the fast-fleeting dog teams left the bank below the town and, lightly harnessed to lightly-loaded sleds, dashed swiftly on and on after the leaders. By two o'clock full fifty sleighs had departed, the last finding the route very plainly shown, where the steel runners had cut a furrow deep in the hard blue ice.

Berry and Tollmarche were together, and ran swiftly by the side of or behind their sled. There was not space on the narrow, foot-high vehicle for blankets, provisions, and themselves. Besides, they only had three dogs.

"Did you get a tent, Tollmarche?" said Berry, as he flicked the leader, who lagged.

"No," replied his companion; "didn't have time. But I've got an axe, and brought the old Yukon stove from our cabin. I think we have enough grub, but it's going to be fearfully cold."

The perspiration mounted to his forehead, though it was 45° below, with just a breath of wind. Running eight miles an hour, not to let your dogs get away from you, is warm work.

The dogs sped on, lapping snow from the side-drifts without stopping. Tollmarche threw himself prone on the ever-moving sleigh. Breathing hard, he clung there a few minutes while it swung around the sharp curves caused by ice hillocks in the trail, the rear pole held by Berry as a rudder. But, fatigued as Tollmarche was, it was colder yet riding on the frozen tarpaulin that covered their supplies, so he soon rolled off into the snow, and, springing to his feet, raced forward, while Berry flung himself in turn on the fleeing sled behind the panting dogs.

The Aurora wavered, shot its starry, glistening shafts athwart the brightening horizon, and gently, like a brilliant rainbow, vanished. The stars, shining far more clearly here than in lower latitudes, were yet, one by one, driven from the firmament by the slow advance of the invisible sun. Daylight, but not sunrise, came; the birch, spruce, and cottonwood-trees surmounting the banks and covering the islands were doubtfully visible through the moving rifts of the fog. A denser mist marked the water-holes in the ice, carefully avoided by the trail; but where the river was wide and straight the narrow pathway led directly through the middle on the ice between the banks of snow.

At 11 A.M., having made fifty-five miles, Berry and Tollmarche found the route left the Yukon and turned up a small tributary to the right, or east. This was more difficult going. The well-defined river track led away to St. Michaels, 1,600 miles distant, and was daily, almost hourly, travelled; but on this little river the untouched snow lay 5 feet deep. The sleds of the stampeders who preceded them had trampled it down on the ice; but yet small, soft hillocks projected here and there, and the weary dogs panted and barked as they jumped the sleigh by a united effort over the obstacles.

In an hour they arrived at camp, and found Daugherty's tent surrounded by fifty-four sleds and innumerable dogs. His sleigh was in the centre, like a Roman general's in the middle of the night's encampment. He and his party were invisible, for they were soundly sleeping in their tent, covered by heavy wolf and lynx robes, while the Malamutes, curled up in a circle tail to nose, lay comfortably in their beds of soft snow.

There were a few stampeders who had no tent, and Berry was of these. He cut down several small spruce-trees, and, dragging the dry branches to a space which Tollmarche had already cleared of snow, speedily made a fire. The little stove was set up; beans and bacon warmed and cooked. They had bread. The dogs were not to be fed until evening, so there was nothing else to do but try to sleep. Now they missed the tent. Within its folds the Yukon stove yields a generous warmth, and, after the snow has been cleared away, by spreading the blankets on top of a few dried boughs one can rest quite comfortably. But when there is no tent it is like trying to warm the whole atmosphere, for the heat is quickly dissipated in the keen air.

Men do not borrow from each other on stampedes. If one is unable to go on because of something lacking, why, it leaves more chances and ground for the others. It is not a question of friendship — it is one of justice. Those who go must be ready. Of course, no one would be left to starve, but they can turn back and go home again.

So it was that Berry and Tollmarche did not sleep, but kept the fire going, piling on wood all the long day; but no sleep.

At seven of the night, the increasing smoke that went directly up into the windless air over the central tent told that the occupants were preparing supper for men and dogs. The camp was at once astir. Billy Chappell came out, and, tying the eight Malamutes separately to adjacent brush, set before each one a large tin bowl heaped full of hot bacon and rice boiled together. It was a scalding though appetizing mixture, and the dogs ate and drank it eagerly but with great care. Occasionally there was a sharp yelp as one, more ravenous than wise, dropped a piece of hot bacon which had burnt his mouth. No matter how friendly these brutes may be with each other, their friendship ceases at meal-time. The wolf blood in their veins asserts itself, and there would be ceaseless fighting over each other's food were they not always tied during that period; but they eat all that is given, and are not fed again for twenty-four hours, except for what few fragments they may find around the camp-fires; and these are infrequent, for your Arctic traveller throws away very little food. Pork, bacon, flour, and beans, are boneless, and no one fails to eat his share of all that has been cooked. Food is too heavy and precious to be wasted in these winter days.

Jim Daugherty was a tall, stalwart, handsome fellow, erect and energetic. The year before he had been to London and the Continent, where he dissipated a goodly little fortune that he had acquired by selling his original locations; for Jim was one of the earliest "sourdoughs," and wandered up and down the Alaskan forests ten years ago, when the existence of gold on the Yukon was almost unknown. Now he was back again, buoyant with the hope of gaining another competency; his reputation was good, and men believed in and followed him. He had "grub-staked" four or five prospectors – furnished them, that is to say, with the outfit and provisions necessary for their researches, and the report of one of these gold-seekers prompted Jim to go with his friends to the place indicated and stake claims.

At nine, with the crystalline moon beaming brilliantly on the placid snow, the camp broke up, and Jim took the lead on foot, the dogs following. Presently he turned to the north-east, and climbed a cañon full of drifted snow. Each man had to take from the sleigh all he could carry, and stagger with it up the ascent; for the eight dogs could scarce drag the empty vehicle. It was not that it was so very steep, but the snow, 6 feet deep, fell on and around them as fast as it was trampled down.

Quite a number of the whole party now went ahead of the first sled, and opened a trail through the snow, using boughs as shovels. On a level this would have been well enough, but on this sharp incline the snow rolled down and back, again and again. It was impossible for the dogs to pull the sled unless the snow was thrown aside, for they would flounder until they were invisible in its depths.

The labour was very harassing, and the men would fall breathless on the snow, reckless of the fact that it was so cold that the icy particles from the breath froze in tiny fragments to their beards and moustaches till they looked, in their fur coats, like white polar bears. The passage of one sled made it easier for the others. So every one helped to move the first half-dozen, and then returned for the rest. There was no question of running away now. All were friends until the summit was attained; for it would not do to leave a single man in that defile – he might never come back. The Arctic pioneers were sometimes selfish, perhaps, as are other men, but always gallant, generous, and chivalrous to a comrade or stranger in danger or distress.

By midnight all were on the summit, and the descent began. This was easy, for the dogs dashed down the hill, floundering through the snowdrifts and whisking the sleighs after them, sometimes over fallen trees, sometimes shooting between them. At times the sled would wedge, and the dogs were held as in a leash, howling, until the breathless men caught up and released the light frame. No one remained on the sleds, and no one directed the dogs. All scrambled down in a mad rush to reach the bottom, and if the ropes got loose and part of a load fell, the owners, who were always in the rear, picked it up and pushed on. A few grasped the steel runners from behind, and, throwing themselves prone on the snow, to act as rudders, let the dogs go; but it was difficult tobogganing, and not one held on to the finish. It was a merry rush withal, and in the little valley below the stampeders stopped to camp and rest. Poor Tollmarche was well-nigh exhausted, and when the reaction came felt cold and sleepy.

"I would go back if I could," he said. "Nonsense," replied his sturdy companion. "We will go on now, if it takes a leg. They say Daugherty is going to stay here all day, so we may get a little rest."

The untiring Klondiker took the axe, and shortly had a bright fire blazing, the snow cleared away on one side, and coffee boiling on the little stove, while Tollmarche threw himself heavily down and listlessly watched the embers and smoke.

A group gathered around him.

"Well," said Will Fisher, clad in a heavy sweater, with moccasined feet and ear-laps thrown up over his fur cap, "I was six weeks coming from Bennett to Dawson early last spring, and we camped out every night, but I never felt so cold and used up as now."

"They say Daugherty is going to freeze us out," said Jim Hall. "He says there are too many, and his friends won't have a fair show."

"I'm ready to quit," said John Scouse. "I thought it might take a day or so only; but I can't stay out a week. I've got to be on Eldorado. Damn these stampedes, anyway! I'd never started if someone hadn't told me Skiff was going. There never was any gold found down this way, and I've been here since '95."

"Yes," said Fisher, "you staked on Eldorado, and are all right, but I'm not. You have something – I've nothing. I was somebody in Frisco. I lost it and came here. This is my fourth stampede. Perhaps it's like the others, but all the same I'm going to the end. I must pay for three sixes."

Tollmarche listened wearily. He thought of India, Burma, his tiger-hunting experiences while in the army, his lost fortune and his present existence and hopes. Retrospection is seldom cheerful or composing.

Meanwhile Berry, himself born in India, bustled around as if he were getting ready for a polo-match at Delhi. He was ever a philosopher – sometimes at other people's expense.

The two men, after eating, slept in the open by the huge fire, with the dogs cuddling on top of the robes for mutual warmth. Even if death ensued, they had to sleep. But others walked about, keeping a kind of guard, and no one suffered.

Daugherty and his three friends, in their comfortable tent, warmed by a large Yukon stove, slept calmly and happily, and never moved camp until next day. They had ample supplies and could linger.

Early the next morning quite a number left for Dawson. During the day it became known that they had been led an unnecessary journey, for it was seen that the valley in which they were camped came directly from the river, and could have been reached without making the terrible climb up and over the icy pass; therefore it was plain that Jim might keep them out a week. The hunt was too long, cold and difficult, with only a faint chance of succeeding, so when the eight Malamutes started away at noon but little more than one-half the party followed the trail.

Berry and Tollmarche were of these, the latter refreshed and stronger, though lacking sleep. It is very hard to sleep without a tent in a temperature of 50° below zero, when one has to replenish the fire every hour.

During the afternoon the course lay up the valley for a number of miles. While the route was harassing, it was not so fearfully wearying as the dash of two days previously. As they left the river littoral, trees were more numerous, both fallen and upright, for the former seemed to be nearly as common as the latter. In time the dead trees and branches would rot, the more quickly for the spring meltings, and make that velvet moss covering of the earth, 2 feet thick, that pervades the whole of primeval Alaska. The spruce-trees were not large. No great specimens were visible; but the young trees grew so closely that once in a while the axes had to cut them down by the dozen to make a passage even for the narrow sledges.

In the late twilight of the wan wintry day a halt was made.

"Well," said Tollmarche, as he unpacked, while Berry cut chips for the stove fire, "I'm happy."

"Why?" said Berry.

"Look," answered Tollmarche, displaying a small six-by-eight tent. "I borrowed this from John Scouse, who, you know, has returned to Dawson. He doesn't need it, as he is not going to stop until he gets there, and he threw it under the tarpaulin as we started. We're all right now, and will follow them to hell."

But that was not necessary. On the fourth afternoon, when they had traversed something over 100 miles of Arctic wastes, Jim Daugherty left his sled at the entrance to a deep glen, which led to the northeast. With Chappell, Skiff and Anderson he broke a path through the heavy snow-drifts that in these defiles lie much deeper than on the level ground. The others followed. After a couple of miles he came suddenly to a small tree, which had been trimmed where it stood down to 4 feet from the ground. The sides near the top had been squared, and on them appeared some words written in pencil.

"This is my south-west stake," said Jim to his companions. "Now, Skiff, go back 500 feet and stake. You, Charley, go up 500 feet and stake; and you can go, Billy, north or south and stake adjoining to Skiff or Charley, as you think best."

The stampeders had all gathered in a group, and watched the proceedings in silence. It was the etiquette of the Klondike that the immediate friends of the discoverer, those who accompanied the sled, had the first privileges next to Discovery on either side, if they chose. Afterwards, for the rest, it was everyone for himself. But it did not always follow that the best claims were nearest Discovery. For while gold is where one finds it, yet its being found in one place on a creek does not preclude the whole creek from being auriferous. That was usually the case, and it very often occurred that many properties proved ultimately richer than the original find.

Jim forced his way to the middle of the snowy glen. After looking about a bit, he pushed the snow aside and disclosed a shaft about 5 feet in diameter, filled with snow.

"Boys," he said, "this shaft is 15 feet to bedrock, and from the bottom we ran a little drift about 10 feet as a cross-cut. The pay runs about 25 cents to the pan for 5 feet. The bedrock pans a dollar on an average for a foot or more. So, you see, if it holds out, and runs up and down the creek, we have a Bonanza here."

"No, I don't know which side is best," he continued in answer to queries. "You have to take your choice; only you know we have come up from the mouth a good two miles, and now the valley is narrowing a bit. I've been in this country off and on for ten years, and my experience is that the gold is concentrated where the creek is not wide; so that the upper half of a gulch ought to be richer than the lower half, all things being equal. You see, the gold, wherever it was originally, certainly comes down, not up, the glen, and is apt to stick nearest the top. In Eldorado, Nos. 97 and 33, miles up from the mouth, are the richest claims.

"Or take Bonanza Creek, twenty-five miles long from the Klondike to Carmack's Forks. Now, from Discovery about halfway up, down to the mouth, how many claims are good? Not more than half a dozen out of a hundred. The valley is too wide and the gold too scattered. Those grounds can only be dredged or hydraulicked, and that will not be for years, for expenses must be reduced and appliances increased. But above Discovery to Carmack's every mine is more or less productive. From 26 above a million has been extracted, and I think there are others there not yet touched that are just as good. Therefore, boys, I'd locate above us if I were you."

It was a long address from reticent, retiring Jim Daugherty, full of good sense and mining philosophy. The man was changed. The surly, almost brutal fellow, who left Dawson like an escaping felon, was by now a good-natured, talkative miner, telling his auditors all he knew. For it might have been that someone would have discovered his shaft and located. There were many mysterious alterations in locations in these early days, and the Gold Commissioner's office was noted for mistakes which it was difficult, if not impossible, to correct.

But his claim was safe now, and so were the locations being made by his friends, Chappell, Anderson, and Skiff. To those who had traced, hunted, and followed him to the lair, he had only kind wishes for their endurance and courage, and he concluded by saying:

"I hope every one of you will find a better property than mine."

Berry and Tollmarche cut four stakes from small trees with their axes, each 4 feet long and 4 inches wide. On the flattened surfaces of one end was written their names, the date of location, and the number of the claim above or below Discovery. The stakes were then driven into the ground at the four corners of the location they had selected. This extended 500 feet, approximately, with the stream, and from side to side of the valley, so that it was a good bit of ground if gold existed in quantities. Later the Government reduced the number of feet that could be located to 250 feet, or one-half. After all had established their rights on the spot, there was another wild rush back to Dawson. It was just as well to have one's location recorded in the Gold

Commissioner's office. Errors were frequent and irritating. No man felt safe until he had the document from that official, duly signed and acknowledged, in his possession.

The remaining stampeders returned without mishap, but, sad to say, all the hardship and struggle went for almost naught. The creek proved a failure, and the locations lapsed again to the Crown the following summer, as the necessary assessment work was not done. Stampedes, like most enterprises in the world, are not all successes. Of twenty that occurred during my first year and a half, not one was more than partially good. Still, it was the uncertainty that attracted. Eldorado and Bonanza were staked on a stampede, and every one hoped that the next rush might disclose equal treasures, and reward its participants with similar wealth.

Chapter 10

THE FIRE

At eight o'clock on the night of April 26, 1899, I came down town from my cabin. I had gone home after an early dinner at the restaurant, and was returning to the warehouse. Passing Monte Carlo, the largest building in Dawson, I observed smoke issuing from the half of the second storey fronting the street. A few seconds later someone cried out 'Fire!' as a thin red flame shot out like a serpent's tongue from one of the upper windows. That was a fearful sound to utter on that cold winter's night! more dreadful than storm or hidden rocks to the seaman. In a moment the street was thronged, packed. Monte Carlo was in the centre of the principal block – the heart of Dawson. Adjoining on both sides were other places of like character, from all of whose portals poured the gamblers and loafers – men and women.

"Where are the engines?" shouted a man.

"Down on the river," replied another voice. "Come down, all of you, and help to stretch the hose."

Down the steep bank and over the frozen river rushed hundreds, eager, fighting to do some good, some service.

By public subscription, a couple of steam-engines had been purchased and brought to Dawson last October just before the freeze-up. One was small; but from the other we expected great service, as it was of the latest model, and supposed to be perfect and complete in every detail. Both engines were stationed on the river ice and covered by double tents. A large hole had been excavated through the ice, 10 feet down to the flowing water beneath. When this aperture was closed by the ice, as occurred every six or seven days, the apparatus was moved to another point a few feet distant, and a second hole dug. So there were numerous little mounds like small pyramids clustered together on the river ice about 100 yards from shore, extending down the stream. A man was supposed to be always there, and to keep a fire in the boilers perpetually. But, alas! there had been some trouble in the local council as to the pay of the four or five men who were engaged as firemen, and when the foremost of the crowd came to the engines there was neither fire nor firemen.

But these Klondikers were men of resource. Some ran back to the shore, and, gaining access to the stores, returned in haste with cans of kerosene, while others carried dry birch and sawdust, which make quick and fierce fires. There was not a pound of coal, except a little blacksmith's coal, in the whole country. The hose was unrolled, stretched, and carried with a hurrah, from the engines, along the river ice, and up the steep bank, the nozzles resting in the middle of the narrow street waiting for water. But the fire had waited for no one.

In this cold latitude the buildings are excessively inflammable. The intense heat of the big fires in the big stoves, that are never extinguished all the winter long, thoroughly dries the log walls and floor, lumber and timber, that make the building. The roof is covered with moss a foot thick, which when dried forms a good covering and coating against ice and cold. But this moss dries – indeed, almost evaporates – near the chimney, where the latter emerges from the roof. The chimney itself, made of thin sheet-iron, is worn through by spring-time. Nothing that man can frame can endure the continual action of fire.

The flames increased in number and size; the smoke obscured the clear starlit sky; window-sashes burst, and gallons of liquor flowed from the broken packages within to the side-walk without, only to be at once frozen in the open air, for it was 45° below zero. The street was enwrapped in a thick fog, so dense that the huge flames, flashing vertically – for there was no wind – could be seen only like lightning gleams. It was remarkable that the heat as well as the flames ascended. The atmosphere was so dry and cold that heat was immediately dissipated, and men that night stood so close to flames as to have their fur clothes burned and destroyed without appreciably feeling the scorching. The area of the fire increased, and the whole block was evidently doomed. People, both men and women, were running with articles in their hands or on their backs to the vacant frozen marsh in the rear, covered with snow. I walked leisurely to my warehouse, which stood apart like an isolated castle, for I knew that it was safe; and I congratulated myself on my expensive fore-thought, for this night was my reward.

At last, at last! the frenzied efforts of the men at the fire-engine had sent water through the frozen hose from beginning to end, and a great cheer went up amid the fog and flames as a small stream of water spurted feebly from the nozzle. But the temperature was 45° below zero, and the line of hose was 400 feet long, lying exposed on the river ice. The power from the engine was not strong enough or not sufficiently developed, and the water slackened gradually until it stopped altogether.

"My God! the water is freezing in the hose," cried someone.

In fact, the water in the hose, from engine to nozzle, had turned into solid ice. Though at various points the expansion of the water when freezing had torn the hose as if with giant scissors, yet the ice remained smooth and compact without breaking, even where the gap in the hose permitted it to be seen. Men gazed at each other through the icy films pendent from eyelashes and eyebrows.

"What is to be done?" shouted Tom Chisholm to Captain Starnes, who commanded the police patrol.

"Blow up the buildings in front of the fire," was the prompt response.

"But where shall we get powder or dynamite?"

"I know," said Schoff, the druggist. "The A.C. has a fifty-pound box of Giant powder in Warehouse A."

"Take a dog team and go for it," ordered Captain Starnes, turning to Sergeant-Major Tucker.

Sergeant Tucker was the most agile, alert, and handsome non-commissioned officer in the whole Yukon body of North-West Mounted Police. Everyone knew and everyone loved as well as respected him. Impervious to interest or friendship while discharging his duties, he was always cautious and competent. The officers' guild will be honoured by the admission of such a "ranker" as Tucker, and I hope the date will not be long delayed. The head of the United States Army, General Young, is a "ranker," and we are ashamed neither of him nor of his career.

"Very well, sir," responded Tucker.

With a crack of the whip the patrol team of three dogs darted like an arrow down the narrow side-street, between the ruddy fires now casting colours above and beyond, while Tucker and Brainard crouched side by side on the sleigh. A voice, and the dogs stopped as suddenly as they started in front of Warehouse A, 200 yards distant. A word to the alarmed and expectant watchman. He remembered the box. It was found, carefully placed on the sleigh, and in ten minutes Sergeant Tucker saluted Captain Starnes, adding:

"There is the box of dynamite, sir."

"Are there any miners here who know how to use Giant powder?" cried Starnes.

"Ay, ay, sir!" came from a score of throats; for the crowd included miners from California and South Africa, to whom firing dynamite was as familiar as lighting their pipes.

Starnes selected McMahon, Thilwall, Armstrong, and Olsen.

"Take the box," he hurriedly said; "open it, and blow up the Aurora, Alex McDonald's building, and the Temenos."

These were three large cabins of two storeys each, right in the pathway of the blaze. For hours hundreds of men had been rushing to the marsh carrying goods from these buildings, but thousands of dollars in value still remained in them. Men were offered 10 dollars an hour, a two-horse team and driver 100 dollars an hour. But even these "Klondike prices" did not secure adequate assistance. Everyone was helping himself or his friend. No one was idle that fateful night. But the buildings had to go.

A few minutes later, and the explosions overswept the fire, scattering fragments far out on the white serene shroud of the frozen Yukon. The miners did their work well, and the fire lagged, for on that side it had nothing more to eat.

Meanwhile I stood at my warehouse door. My horses were ready harnessed. I had three double teams, and could have had 500 dollars for the night's work. But I preferred to offer them to my friends. The warehouse was filling with merchandise, hurried thither on wagons, sleighs, horses' backs, dogs' backs, men's backs. The large door was quickly opened, the stuff pitched inside, and the door again closed without delay.

My porter came to me as I stood with thousands of others grouped around, watching the fire, and whispered, "Do you remember the twenty cases of gasolene?" I did remember. At this moment men were on the wooden roof of the warehouse throwing buckets of water and ice on old tarpaulins spread over the sliding surface. The water was found by smashing the ice that covered the many pools on the marsh. Near the bottom was always some water. Thousands of sparks were flying towards us, making the air red and white, and shooting in at the door when opened.

There was a big Irishman helping me whom I knew on the Comstock in Nevada. I had promised him work whenever I controlled a mine, and now, like a Titan, he was wielding the buckets of water and ice. I called him softly: "Dennis." He came. I was standing at the door, which I opened, then pulled him inside and shut it again. Dragging him to the pile of gasolene and lighting a match, I hurriedly said:

"Dennis, here are twenty cases of gasolene. If it remains we shall be blown up, and if it is known outside there will be a panic."

"What do you want me to do?"

"Take it out quietly, go to the rear of the warehouse fifty yards back, and throw the cases in the snow. If they then explode, no one nor nothing will be hurt."

He picked up two cases, one under each arm, weighing 90 pounds each, and followed me in the darkness to the door, which I opened, and he fled. In a few seconds he was back, breathless, with another stalwart companion, and in ten minutes the dangerous liquid was lying in 5 feet of snow, where I found the cases next day safe enough.

All this time the fire was roaring nearer, leaping towards us with eager strides, and striving enviously to bridge the few feet of ice and frost between it and my refuge. But the distance was enough, and it gradually died out from starvation, leaving sputtering jets here and there on the wide desolation of blocks and streets. I opened my stores and gave wine and whisky to whosoever came – and they were many – for I felt relieved and grateful.

Around me were thousands of men and women struggling with articles saved from the fire, some putting up little shelters, and others sitting, cast down and forlorn, on the goods they had snatched from the burning. The entire city seemed gone, and yet the quantity of stuff rescued was surprising. The white marsh for hundreds of feet was littered with everything necessary in a Klondiker's outfit – tools, provisions, clothing, furs. One wondered how anything could be lost; yet the amount was said to be near two million dollars.

The next day everything in the burnt district lay prone, except a number of huge piles composed of square blocks of ice. Within the previous weeks the larger institutions had cut and transported from the river-bed these blocks of ice for summer use. They had been saturated with sawdust, and a wooden shelter erected. The sawdust, shelter, buildings, all were gone; but the ice remained – the only thing that had passed through the heat with impunity. Extraordinary as it seemed, the piles served in some cases as lines of demarcation to the owner's land. For that very afternoon, before the embers were entirely cold, people began to bring lumber and rebuild. Lumber doubled in value that same day.

Still the "sourdoughs" were making comparisons with the fire of 1897. It would seem that Dawson was to have its annual big fire, not to count the little ones. "Why," said Jim McNamee, when told that lumber had advanced from 100 dollars to 200 dollars a thousand, "that's nothing. I remember, after the fire in December, 1897, that nails sold for 25 cents each. Men delved in the ashes, broke up old boards and boxes, dismantled old doors and sluices, for nails. There were only a few kegs in town, and they sold for 250 dollars each keg. A man with a bucket full was like one with a good pan of gold. Talk about lumber at 200 dollars! why, you couldn't get any then. The lumber-mill was burnt in the fire, and there was none nearer than Circle City, 300 miles away. We just had to whip-saw it. We had to cut the trees near town up there on the mountains," indicating a bare point, "make a pit in the ice, and whip-saw for all we was worth. I tell you that was hard. Two men couldn't do no more than 100 feet, and then it'ud be filled with knots, and sometimes split in the cold when you druv a little nail in it. And beans and bacon wuz a dollar, flour 40 dollars a sack, and moccasins! – you just had to make 'em yourself out of old clothes, for they wasn't any to be had. Talk about lumber at 200 dollars! Why, you fellows ain't in it; you don't know what hard times is!" And Jim stalked away growling his disgust. This is always the way; the past and the future are worse than the present, which, indeed, is not always unpleasant.

One of the banks had possessed a steel vault, enclosing several safes. The log building was quickly destroyed, leaving the vault standing, but as the fire grew more intense the expansion of the hot air caused the vault sides to be blown open, and threw out a stream of golden sovereigns 20 feet away, like soapsuds from a boy's pipe. Watches, gold-dust, jewelery, twenty-dollar pieces – all that was on the wooden shelves of the vault – were mingled and fused in a molten mass. For days and nights subsequently a guard from the barracks stood around a roped space while the ground was dug, scraped, and washed, as in a mine, for the precious metals and jewels that had been scattered far and wide. The three safes, though sunk a foot in the thawed soil, seemed intact, and when opened were found to have preserved even the paper money unburnt – a sum running into the hundreds of thousands. The safes were also full of gold in bars and dust, amounting to nearly 2,000,000 dollars. They weighed something like 2 tons each and I was asked to move them to a safe place.

I waited until the next night, when the crowd that hung around all day would be dispersed. Then, with my horses, sleighs, and men, I took them down to the Alaska Commercial Company's strong log building that had, fortunately, been preserved. It was a very difficult thing to do, for the sleds broke repeatedly under the immense concentrated weight, besides sinking deep into the ground. The fire had broken up the frost for 2 feet, and while the intense cold of the day had frozen the surface again, yet the ground beneath had had no time to harden, and the sleds went down as in a bog. We had no ropes of sufficient strength, only two crowbars, and were forced to make wooden rollers for the safes. It took all night, but we finally succeeded in landing them safely in the A. C., and at eight o'clock I went to bed, feeling entitled to a rest after forty-eight hours' ceaseless labour and anxiety.

Chapter 11

THE MINE

After my return from the journey to the mines I looked around seriously for some future occupation. My flour and other merchandise would presently be sold. Competition was increasing, prices decreasing, as each day wafted us closer to the spring sunshine and the open river teeming with steamers. The flour was purchased from me largely in ten-sack lots by bakers, of which guild there was a number in Dawson. While the miner could cook his porridge and meat, yet he could not with baking-powder make bread on his narrow stove as white, light, and soft, as that of the baker; so, as the bakers' prices were relatively moderate, quantities of their flour were consumed.

One cold day a boy, with five dogs yoked tandem to his sled, came with an order from a baker for ten sacks of flour. While the porter was piling it on the sled, I said to the boy.

"I have been over in your country."

"What's that?" he replied.

"I've been over in your country," I repeated; "I've been to Yokohama, Tokio, and Nagasaki. What part of Japan did you come from?"

"Why, what do you take me for?" he brusquely ejaculated.

"For a Japanese, of course," I said.

"I ain't no Japanese; I'm a full-blooded Indian, and no Japanese," he sternly repeated, drawing himself together.

I was amazed. "Where in the world did you learn English so well?" I gasped.

"At the missionary school at Holy Cross, on the Lower Yukon," he responded; and, gathering the dogs up from the snow, where they lay in supreme content, he surlily lashed them off to the familiar refrain of "Mush! Mush! Mush!"

I leave the above to the ethnologists. If ever I saw a Japanese in Yokohama, that Indian boy of the Yukon was one. Sturdy, stocky, short, broad-chested, with narrow long eyes and swarthy skin, he looked a Japanese of the Japanese, and yet he was a full-blooded Indian.

It is easy to remember thereafter that the Behring Strait is not much more than thirty miles wide, and is frozen solid every winter. From wherever may have come the aborigines of lower America, I know not, but the Alaskan Indians are descended from the Japanese, and not so very remotely. That boy could have walked the streets of Tokio without attracting the slightest attention. I am convinced no one would have thought him other than an ordinary Japanese coolie. And he was not an Eskimo living on the seashore, but came from one of the river tribes, and where he was taught English is 500 miles from Behring Sea. The dogs he drove that day were of the pure Malamute stock – that is, "inside" dogs, those raised on the Yukon.

The "outside" dogs are of all breeds, brought in by "cheechakas" from everywhere. Scotch collies, English bull-dogs, St. Bernards, Great Danes, Newfoundlands – they pervaded the Klondike in endless variety. Every miner had a couple, and the larger mines a dozen. Each shop in Dawson kept a tandem of at least two dogs, attached to a sled in front of the shop, ready to deliver merchandise round town when sold. Three dogs on the level roads and up comparatively steep grades, with a lightly-built sleigh and some assistance, could easily transport 500 pounds. They will go at a dog-trot on a level snow trail all day long with this load, making forty to sixty miles.

The "outside" dogs become acclimatized very rapidly, Nature providing a shaggy hair covering even for the Great Danes. Their value, however, is not quite so high or permanent as that of an average Malamute. A good Malamute will sell for 150 dollars, while it must be a very superior "outside" dog that will bring more than 100 dollars. But the leader is always a small "outside" dog, usually of the Scotch collie breed. These are very intelligent, and possess to a marked degree the faculty of nosing out the narrow trail, even when covered with a foot or two of new snow. The leader is not supposed to add much to the pulling power. It is his duty to keep the trail and hold the harness taut. He obeys orders with more promptitude and discipline than a horse, and is really the leader of the team in brains as well as position. As soon as he hears the faint cries of "Whoa!" which tell him that his master has been thrown out and is wrestling with the snow, he stops so suddenly that often the other dogs with the sleigh come tumbling over him, a snarling, biting mass. He alone never moves, but crouches silently on the trail, awaiting his driver's coming and word of command. Without dogs we could scarcely have existed this winter. They were invaluable in the absence of horses and feed, which was costly also, and then not good.

The next winter found us with plenty of red-topped, wild hay, cut from the valleys and hillsides of Bonanza and other creeks tributary to the Klondike, and it was quite nutritious. Moreover, we learned this winter the degree of cold that horses could endure and survive. Major Steel told me that horses belonging to the North-West Mounted Police had been turned out in the early winter in Manitoba, and in spring when taken up were found to be in good condition, though the thermometer had descended to 30° below during the season.

In November, 1898, horses were left to die on the trails and in Dawson. There was neither work nor feed for them. Horses were offered to me for their keep, but I refused. Those same horses wandered up in the hills where the snow was 5 feet deep on the hillsides. They brushed the snow away with feet and nose, finding luscious whortleberries, blackberries, and raspberries, in great quantities. These are, in fact, the staple food of the bear in winter. The berries, with the red-topped grasses growing under the snow 3 and 4 feet high, made a succulent and fattening food. The lowest authentic record at the barracks was 57° below zero, yet in the spring the horses were reclaimed by their owners, and looked infinitely better than when turned out to die at the commencement of winter. This was a lesson as well as a revelation.

During the summer of 1899 horses were imported into the Klondike in numbers, and 1,200 of them passed the next winter in transporting men and supplies from Dawson to the mines. The dogs were almost entirely superseded, and their value became merely nominal; for a good horse, after all, could pull a ton over the smooth icy trails – a labour that would require three sleighs and twenty dogs. Such is the difference between the applied strength of the two. The horse is built for strength, the dog for activity.

While residing and doing business in Dawson, I never omitted to examine any reasonably good mining proposition. In order to understand the topography of the whole Klondike mining area, I made my winter journey of eleven days, in January, 1899, over the whole extent of the mining creeks. It gave me a crude but hasty knowledge both of the method of winter working and the different relative values of various districts. This, however, I supplemented by speedy trips to individual mining properties when offered for sale. No matter how distant the mine or cold the weather, if I thought at least some knowledge might be acquired, I engaged a driver and started with dogs. I never could drive them successfully, and still less feed them, though I had actually come to enjoy the breathless trot behind the sleigh for half a mile, and then the sweet, contented rest, when I threw myself panting on the never-stopping vehicle for five minutes – no more.

All the furs in the world will not keep one warm in a passive attitude out in the Arctic air at 50° below. Though the body may be bathed in perspiration from exercise, yet the ears, nose and fingers chill so quickly that it is dangerous to lie or sit in the sleigh. In this atmosphere, however, one never becomes fatigued, and one is always hungry – two good requisites for health. Some day invalids will be sent to the Arctic regions to spend a winter as they are now ordered to Egypt. Only the desert winter air is comparable with the Arctic winter atmosphere. The dryness and purity of both are to be found in few other places on the globe.

By these several journeys, which seldom lasted more than two days, I acquired a very definite plan of the better as well as the poorer localities. In addition I learned the ways of working mines in the winter, and thought they could be vastly improved. Indeed, I felt myself quite an expert, for I was aware that few had travelled and investigated as much as myself to gain both a technical and practical knowledge of mines and mining.

In February, 1899, I again left Dawson to examine a mining property. The distance, thirteen miles, I traversed on foot in three hours, over a beautiful trail of solid snow and ice, passing a continual stream of men, dogs, and horses, who were going and coming. The sun was clear and high, and, though it was excessively cold, the leaves, which never seem to desert the bushes and birch-trees, glistened dazzlingly with the pendent icicles. Every one had a dog or two, and the custom that I had seen in the fall, of men stooping under 100 pounds' weight of tools and provisions, had disappeared. Those going to town naturally had no freight, and the tinkling of the merry sleigh-bells, heard before the dogs dashed wildly and recklessly round the sharp curve in front, warned me to leap as quickly off the narrow five-foot trail into the soft snow that made a border of white lilies along the hillsides ahead and behind. The dogs are not driven with a line, and, going with an empty sleigh to Dawson, where they know warm food and the amorous company of other dogs await them, they rush as if the devil were after them. From the Grand Forks to Dawson, a distance of fifteen miles, has been made frequently by dog teams in an hour and a quarter.

I arrived at the base of Cheechaka Hill, overhanging Bonanza, in the afternoon, and climbed through the snow to the little cabin which I knew was my goal, situated about two-thirds up the slope. I cannot remember a more fatiguing half-hour in my experience. The snow was only 4 or 5 feet deep, but yet it was difficult going, and all kinds of creepers and cut tree-stumps entrapped my weary feet. Moreover, the slight warmth of a February afternoon sun had partly melted and yet hardened the top of the snow, so that it resembled glassy thin ice. Once and again my feet went from under me, and I "came a whacking cropper," sliding down several yards until my frantic grabs caught hold of something.

It was a most woebegone Klondiker who finally knocked at the closed portal of the six-by-eight cabin for admittance, and, when the door was quickly and hospitably opened, fell on the low, dirty, narrow cot in the dark corner. But that seemed as if of downiest feathers, and in a few minutes I had completely recovered. No one has leisure to be lazy in the Klondike. The two men within were employed by the owner at 10 dollars a day, and after I had rested they took me into the mine, which I found consisted merely of a tunnel 80 feet long and 7 feet by 7 in dimensions. The face of the tunnel, as well as the sides, was frozen hard, so hard, indeed, that the sharp and tempered pick, as it struck the unyielding gravel, produced little more than sparks. With difficulty I picked down enough of dirt to fill two gold-dust pans, which I then carried to the cabin, one on top of the other. I thought it just as well to handle them myself. I did not care for "salt" or "sugar" in the dirt; I wanted only that dust which Nature had already provided, if any.

In the cabin was a tub filled with warm water, taken from an iron pot on the stove that was kept filled with ice and snow. Here I learned that melted ice yields five times as much water as the same bulk of snow.

Lowering the two pans on top of one another into the tub, I let them soak for half an hour. By then the warm water had thawed the frozen gravel, so that it could be easily broken with one's hand into mud and stones. I washed out the contents of the pans very carefully, finding a few grains of gold remaining in each. Gold, being the heaviest of all metals, moves least and slowest. These grains I weighed with extreme attention on the small gold scales that are found in every cabin. We three then went out again, and I made a careful inspection of the tunnel and adjoining locations. Having selected two principal points, the men took picks, and with much exertion broke off a small portion of the frozen ground. A quantity of wood was piled close against each of the exposed points, and dirt thrown on top. After tamping, fire was applied. We knew that the wood would burn and smoulder all night, so we waited until next morning. Then one of the men, Long John Twiggs, cleared the ashes and unburnt fragments away. I took a pick, and found that I could easily thrust it in for 6 or 8 inches, such had been the effect of the fire in thawing and disintegrating the gravel. In filling the pans, we found the dirt was yet warm, though the temperature was so low that, having taken off one of my gloves to scrape some of the gravel into a pan, and then grasping the pick without replacing the glove, in less than two minutes the tool and my hand were as one, and the skin came off my thumb, while the other fingers were all blistered when finally my poor hand was released. Extreme cold produces precisely the same effects as extreme heat. A bottle filled with kerosene at 50° below zero burns the hand just as sharply as one filled with boiling water.

Again I carried the pans myself to the little black, dirty, dismal cabin, with its ice and snow shrouds, and never let them beyond my vision until in the melted ice of the tub I again washed the gravel and found once more a few grains of gold-dust. The gold contents of one pan weighed 25 cents, and of the other 28 cents. This was satisfactory, but I was not satisfied. I must make all the tests I could. It would not do to be deceived or to deceive myself. There were other days and other mines in the country, and neither this mine nor any other mine was absolutely necessary. But it was essential to be right and make no mistake, for, besides the loss of money, the time that must be consumed in working a poor property, before one was quite fully convinced of its worthlessness, was in itself invaluable, for each year the good mines would be enhanced in price as their values became better known. Besides, one did not go to the Klondike for ordinary chances – those could be taken or had anywhere; but the man who ostracized himself from the world, who was ready to live on bacon and beans, who separated himself by a wall of ice and snow 600 miles thick from the nearest post or point to which came regular tidings of the world's doings, who was willing to live thus for years – such a man was entitled to expect a recompense somewhat higher than might be vouchsafed the one who remained in those lower latitudes where the birds sing their daily carol, where the sun rises every day, and one can go, if he will, from place to place without either freezing or starving. Therefore I stayed on in the dirty little cabin, which looked as if it had not been swept since it was first occupied. The two berths, one above the other, were small, the stove smaller, and the window smallest of all. The last was constructed of empty pint stout bottles arranged in a circular form, with the mouths pointing inwards, making a round orifice in the log wall about a foot across, through the interstices of which, strange to say, came a good deal of light. Long John told me, when I asked why he did not have a glass window, that, if a six-by-eight could be bought in Dawson at all, it would cost 10 dollars. I said no more on that subject.

We had bacon and beans for dinner, and pork and beans for supper. I could not indicate a special preference for one over the other. The bread was homemade, being, in fact, hot cakes, to be eaten while hot, for they are hard as brick-bats when cold. However, few ever had the chance to cool. With these came tea, coffee, canned corned beef, tomatoes and peas, and evaporated potatoes – the last I never could stomach. Several kinds of food were put up in a condensed form, with all the water evaporated, like the pemmican made for the Arctic traveller. We had, for instance, evapo-rated turnips. All these, though they may have contained ample nutriment, and doubtless served their purpose, were absolutely tasteless and without savour. For the miners, however, in this pioneer winter, these foods were very essential, as several days' supply of them could be carried in a small compass, and they were not, comparatively, so very dear.

The frozen spruce wood split easily under the axe, and made a warm, splendid fire; and after our supper the little dirty cabin seemed quite cosy and cheerful with our ani-mated conversation. We talked of our work in exploring during the day, and what we heard or knew of our neigh-bours' prospects. It is curious, but as I look back and remember the week spent in that lonesome eagle's eyrie on the slope of the icy hillside, our talk was not of home or outside memories, as might naturally be supposed, but our minds were centred on the question of how much gold was in the mines, and the best and cheapest way to extract it.

Fat Dan had been over the whole district more or less, prospecting, and so had I. We compared observations, while Long John listened and learned. It was strange how the wish and purpose to make money had expelled all other thoughts; it was as if the past were a dream. No vocal regrets for being on the Klondike, no laments and longings for the world we had left – we knew it would stay until we returned, and greet us according to our success. Home, friends, life, the banished sunshine, and distant sweethearts – all were forgotten. We thought little of the piercing cold, less of the rude victuals and inhospitable abode. Gold! gold had drawn us to the Arctic solitudes, and the desire of it enwrapped our whole being. We related no stories, laughed at no anecdotes, indulged in no reminiscences, but agreed where we would dig next morning after the burning, and then to bed.

At the end of a week I returned to Dawson, resolved to purchase the undeveloped mine at a reasonable figure. The owner, who had located it just a year before, at a cost of 15 dollars, readily sold it to me for a snug little fortune, and at once left the country. He had been there but a little over a year, and went back blithe and happy to New England, where waited his wife and children. He was one of the lucky ones. I sent a man – not a miner – up there with instructions to employ half a dozen miners. Meanwhile I reduced my affairs in Dawson daily, selling my goods and collecting my accounts. I had seen so many failures of mines in the country for lack of personal supervision that I was fixed in the resolve that, if this enterprise should prove a failure also, why, it should be the fault of the mine, but not of myself.

On May 1 I moved my simple belongings to Cheechaka Hill, and, selling my warehouse in Dawson, settled down to a miner's life. It seemed at first quite pleasant. We worked about a dozen men, and built a warm dining-room, with an adjoining chamber for the cook and his wife, at the base of the hill, upon the margin of the frozen brook; a small addition as an office, with two bunks like those for steerage passengers on an Atlantic liner, served me very well. The men slept in an old cabin which came with the mine.

One day a "sourdough" (old-timer) was employed. They used to say that the genuine pioneer never undressed during the winter. In this case, at least, I cannot say, but I do aver that a committee of the miners waited on the foreman after the "sourdough" had sojourned for a week in the sleeping-cabin, and demanded either his or their discharge – for they said the cabin was never asleep, and the new arrivals loved them so much that they accompanied the men even to the mine. The complaint being unusual, though the condition not unknown, the foreman thought it his duty to refer it to the owner. I felt that the miners were somewhat captious, for the "sourdough" only conformed to the ancient customs and regulations of the North before the "cheechakas" came. Yet, as times change, I could not but acquiesce in their demand, so the "sourdough" was discharged and left, grumbling at the niceties of the "cheechakas." The sleeping-bunks and wooden walls were carefully fumigated, but just so soon as the weather permitted, the men left the structure and lived in small tents that they erected on the hillsides and in the valley.

As the summer advanced and the brilliant sunshine sparkled in the west later and later each evening, flowers appeared and grew luxuriantly with mushroom-like rapidity. Presently the hillsides were completely covered with purple and carmine, and one walked through Nature's garden. Mingled with the daisies and honeysuckles, the violets and geraniums, were sweet grasses. These last made fine provender for the horses. Flour, bread, bacon, grass — everything was champagne and truffles to my horse Jack, whom I had bought from Monroe Salisbury. Jack during the ensuing summer was a splendid scavenger. No dog or vulture in the streets of Constantinople was more diligent or less fastidious. He would eat anything and everything. Each afternoon after his lay-off he would go to the rear of the mess-kitchen. Then would ensue a battle royal with the dogs for the possession of the half-opened and not wholly emptied cans of tomatoes, corn, canned meats of various kinds, and tinned salmon, that were carelessly thrown out of doors by the cook. Jack, after fighting off the dogs, would carefully insert his long tongue between the jagged openings made by the Chinese meat hatchet in the top of the cans, and lick the succulent morsels with infinite gusto and evident contentment. After all were cleaned to the last taste, he would leave reluctantly and regretfully, and browse on the rich grasses concealing the hillsides: stolen fruits were to him the sweetest. The animals, like the people who lived in this land, soon learned to eat any and every thing. There is nothing like a crisp atmosphere and a long day's work to produce an appetite. It's a good place for consumptives and hypochondriacs, not to speak of the indolent. The one becomes well, and the other active.

We started on the hillside two new tunnels, parallel to and equidistant from the old. We did not use the old tunnel, because it was neither in the proper location nor of the proper size. The tunnels, though comparatively dry, yet had to be timbered from the beginning. We sent steam into them through pipes from 1 to 2 inches in diameter. In this, as in everything else, nothing was complete. There was not enough pipe in the country to supply the demand that arose when it was known how much superior was the process of steaming to thawing by wood fires. Our pipe-line was 2 inches, 1½ inches, 1¾ inch, inch, and ½ inch. We made our own reducers, fitted the various sizes to each other, and even made steam-pipe out of rubber garden hose picked up anywhere. Nothing came amiss, and every man had to use his brains as well as his hands. At the end of the drift we pierced the frozen ground by steel points 5 feet long, hollow, with a narrow orifice, from which the steam escaped and struck the granite gravel. By driving the point gently with a wooden mallet, the steam made its way through gravel and rocks, no matter what size. It was marvelous what it could do. In half an hour there would be three holes 4 feet long and an inch wide. The same result under the old process of using hand-drills and iron hammers took seven hours. This improvement was first perfected at our mine, but we asked for no patent. Every miner was allowed to use it, and did so as soon as they knew its great superiority over the "sourdough" method. Into the holes thus excavated were placed extensions of the steam-pipe. The steam issued from the pointed end and percolated through the frozen ground, thawing and disintegrating. It was allowed to remain ten hours, then withdrawn, and the miners, going at once to work, removed the 4 feet of dirt thus loosened. At least twice as much was accomplished thus as by wood-burning, which up to now had been the universal method of working frozen ground in Alaska and the North-West.

Above the tunnels was a marshy bit of ground full of springs, which exhausted the horses and nearly broke my heart. It was simply a bog. Brush and small trees would sink into it like stones when pressed by the wagon wheels. The horses would go down to their bellies, and, after unharnessing, had to be assisted from the quagmires. Yet we struggled on, for if there was no wood the mine would have to stop, and that would never do – anything but that. We had two wagons and a dog-sleigh, the latter of not much use. A day came when my best teamster darkened the open door of the little office. My heart misgave me, for his presence boded misfortune. "What is it, Jim?" I asked.

"The off fore-wheel is broken," he answered.

I knew what that meant, for I had foreseen it. "Badly?" I asked.

"Nearly all the spokes and felloes; besides, the tire is badly bent."

I ran up the hill to the blacksmith's shop. I called Mackenzie, the blacksmith, and John, the foreman. The latter had been a carpenter in Missouri. I told them the situation, which they already knew. Mac said:

"Nothing can be done. In order to weld the tire on, I must have good blacksmith's coal to heat it, and we have scarce a pound. I sent up to the Forks this morning, but even Neilsen, the Swedish blacksmith, has none, or, if he has, he won't give it to us."

"And," added John, "we haven't a felloe. There may be some in Dawson, however."

To Dawson and back meant a whole day. In the meantime the little reserve of wood would be gone, and operations would have to stop. The mine was costing 600 dollars a day, and many expenses could not be curtailed or arrested.

"Well," I finally said, after discussing the situation thoroughly, "we have neither tires, spokes, nor felloes, and we can't buy, beg, borrow, nor steal them. There's only one thing left: we must make them."

"How are you going to do that?" they both exclaimed.

"If we send to Dawson for a tire, spokes, felloes, and coal, it will take a day, even if we get them. But we cannot, must not, stop."

They assented.

"Now," I continued, "can we not build up a wheel solid from the hub without felloes or spokes, and put some horseshoes straightened on for tires?"

Mackenzie said: "I can make the horseshoes do as a tire, I think, but they will be narrower than the wheel."

"No matter," said the carpenter; "I'll get some dry birch and build the wheel solid from the hub in three hours, if you will give me a man to help."

And it was done. The old horseshoes were straightened, and then curved, and then nailed on with horseshoe nails. We thought they would hold better in the soft birch. Then to the crest of the hill we went, tied the horses to the wagon by ropes 20 feet in length, and from their vantage on dry ground they pulled out the crippled wagon. Quickly and deftly was the wheel slipped on to the axle by Mac and John, and when the vehicle was loaded it rolled away after the horses with comparative ease. It is true that the wheel was not exactly circular, nor did it have the same even symmetry as the others, but it did its work well enough, and the wagon procured wood for the boilers.

We made another wheel of like character from an old hub as a reserve, and when the first was broken it made a fair substitute until late in June, when wagons and machinery supplies of every kind arrived down the river from Skagway in abundance.

The same difficulties meanwhile confronted us in our tramway, built at an angle of 45° from between the mouths of the two tunnels to the base on the creek bed where we sluiced the dirt. The two cars were connected by an old Manila rope only an inch in diameter, and each carried a ton when loaded. The loaded car descending brought up the empty, the two passing at a switch about midway. I paid the builder of this tramway an ounce a day, with board. We had neither iron or steel rails nor strap iron of any kind to lay on the tramway, on which to run the wheels. The latter were made of wood, very similarly to the wagon wheel and with the same horseshoe covering. Fortunately, we could buy plenty of the latter. It was rather difficult to make wooden wheels a foot in diameter strong enough to sustain a car with a ton of dirt descending a steep incline on wooden slides, themselves warped, unsteady, and yielding. But we built them by the dozen, and if one broke or was crushed it was at once replaced by another with scarce five minutes' delay.

It was very wearying and harassing to meet and overcome these difficulties, but we had to do it or stop. There was no other alternative, as the necessary supplies would not arrive in Dawson before July, and the summer season was only five months at best. The early pioneers to the frozen North had to cope with unknown and unforeseen troubles.

I employed in and about the mine some fifty men, none of whom was paid less than 5 dollars a day and board; foremen received 10 dollars. I was my own superintendent. During this summer of 1899 the hotels and road-houses charged 3 dollars a day for board. However, we had fresh meat in plenty brought in from the "outside," and I fed them well, for I believe that a man labours better when he is well fed.

Many of the mine-owners paid their employees 8 dollars a day, including board, and let them cook for themselves in their own cabin. It was trying for a miner to warm his mush and coffee over a little fire in his cabin during the early morn, and, after working five hours in a close tunnel, to emerge therefrom wet and muddy, and eat bacon and beans for his mid-day meal. In the evening, after his ten hours' labour, he went to cabin or tent, and then prepared the only good repast of the day; but he was tired, cross, and indisposed to give himself a hearty variety. I have noticed that men who continually growl at the lack of quality and variety of food given by their employers do not always supply themselves with an equal quality and variety when living alone. This is not, however, economy, but fatigue. It cost me a dollar and a half to board the men with everything the markets supplied, especially eggs. These came in crates from far-off Indiana, each crate containing thirty dozen, and cost at the mine about 20 dollars a case. I think, for several weeks after they first began to arrive, and before the men became surfeited, the camp consumed a case and half daily, or a dozen to each man. The poor fellows had only had visions of eggs from last autumn when the river froze. They ate them cooked in manifold ways, but the most common was out of the shell, in the old-fashioned manner. I thought that my miners, with their meals ready to the hour, warm, appetizing and plentiful, did more work than those employed by my neighbours who did not board them.

One day, as a test, I measured tunnels of corresponding dimensions worked by the same number of miners in two of the adjoining mines, and found that we made nearly one-fifth more progress; and I was convinced later that it was even more than that. Certainly, men working for us got ready pay, good feeding, and, if competent, steady employment, which concomitants were lacking in many other properties; still, whether employed by one's self or others, it makes a material difference whether one works only or works and cooks. Cooking is a separate industry, and does not belong to outdoor life.

My cooks were a Frenchman and his wife. He was from Alsace, and spoke French and German with equal facility. He had been a lieutenant in the German army, and a fine figure he must have been with his black eyes, clear face, and military bearing. His wife was very clever. Well educated, speaking English as well as the other two languages, pretty and vivacious, she was the belle of the camp, where, indeed, women were scarcer than gold.

They cooked, washed, cleaned the dishes, waited at table, and chaffed the miners, with as much verve and cheerfulness as if it had been their habitual vocation. To these surroundings everyone had to adapt himself without whining or whimpering. It was no place for laggards.

Not far from our mess-house, to which was attached my office and bunk, stood a cabin of the usual size and make – that is to say, with one door, one window, one room. It was tenanted by a husband and wife and two men. The husband had a "lay," and employed the others. A "layman" is one who works a mine on an agreement with its owner to pay him a specified percentage on the gross output. The wife was a comely, healthy young woman from Oregon, hard-working, without a bit of sentiment. Round a Klondike mining camp all become well acquainted in two or three days. Life moves fast during the summer months, and the amenities of civilization are not always in evidence. She came over one sunny evening to borrow some sugar. Casually I said:

"Do you not find it awkward to sleep in the same room with two other men besides your husband?"

"Oh dear no," she replied; "I'm used to it now. Besides, I put a little curtain before our bed, and then one is an old man whom I knew in Oregon, and the other is a young fellow whom I don't mind. But," she added naively, "it was a little awkward last winter when there were seven of us, you know."

"What!" I exclaimed, "seven of you in one cabin, and only one woman?"

"Yes," she replied; "five men with my husband and myself occupied the same cabin in which we are now living. My husband employed them on his lay up the hill, and I cooked and washed – when there was any washing to be done," she added, with a slight twinkle in her eyes.

"And you all lived in that little cabin?"

"All of us. They were very good, and I didn't mind it after a while. Still, I don't think I would like it again unless we just had to."

I knew that, with all this sacrifice, the winter's output had not been large, and the men were paid only part of their wages. Several of them were then working for me. It was a pity that such devotion to wifely duty had not received more shining rewards.

The summer went on apace, and everyone was busy – a brilliant summer, with little rain, clear skies, and warm, charming atmosphere. The hills were covered with flowers; birds sang in the trees; no one was sick, and all seemed happy and contented. The cold and hardships of the winter were as a mirage. The hills and valleys teemed with eager, strong, active men prospecting, buying, working. The long days seemed too short.

Mirabile dictu! on one of July's latter days a wagon rolled into my camp – a wagon, an actual, genuine wagon – loaded with pumping machinery. We looked at it as we would have gazed upon a mastodon or a balloon. But there it was, a veritable freight wagon with four horses attached, all looking worn and haggard. No wonder; for they had been five days hauling that wagon, with its light load, thirteen miles from Dawson. It was not enough to corduroy a road. The trees had to be cut away, the stumps shortened, the everlasting tufts of moss leveled, and the marsh filled. It took seven men with four horses to transport the wagon to its destination at No. 2 above. It was done, however. Another step for civilization! The road remained; other wagons appeared as unexpectedly as the soldiers of Cadmus, and freight tariffs from Dawson fell from 6 cents to 2 cents, and even less, per pound. Horses hauled wagons instead of "packing" loads, and the vision of men transporting articles of all descriptions on their backs disappeared for ever – at least on Bonanza.

Five thousand men were working within a radius of two miles, and dogs, which had been supposed to be good only during the winter, were now employed in "packing" provisions up the steep hillsides. Little saddle-bags of canvas were made, and a fair-sized dog could "pack" 30 or 40 pounds at the pace of a moderate walk. No one, neither man nor animal, idled that summer on the Klondike.

I went to Dawson very seldom. I did not feel as if I ought to go away, as I was my own superintendent and had plenty to do. We bought wagons and horses, and twice a week sent them to town with orders for articles wanted.

One evening, however, I left the mine on horseback after dinner for Dawson, having in my saddlebags 35 pounds of gold-dust. I took a short cut and led my horse down a steep defile, jumping him across a couple of wide ditches. On mounting I found my saddle-bags gone. They were old, had been tied to the saddle, and had doubtless slipped off. I left the horse loose and retraced my path in a hurry, with a good bit of anxiety. I knew no one had passed me either way, but then they might. Fortunately, as I rushed up the hill, there before me, in the faint moonlight, lay the saddle-bags. The cord had broken, and they had fallen away while the horse was leaping a log. I picked them up, found my horse, tied the bags firmly, and went on.

At Magnet 18 below, the creek was muddy and my horse lost the ford. Weighted with the dust and myself, the animal could not ascend the steep bank, and sank to the middle of his belly in the ooze and water. I stood erect on the saddle like a circus-rider, and, first throwing the bags to the shore, followed myself by a great leap, just escaping by a narrow squeeze a bath in the dirty slime. Even then I had trouble in getting Jack out of what might have been his grave.

I found a good ferry over the Klondike two miles from Dawson. It was a beautiful, clear, cold stream, rushing like a rapid. Fine grayling could be seen darting along 20 feet below the surface.

The many cabins to the left near its junction with the Yukon were empty and deserted. They had only formed a portion of the city of refuge for those who wintered there in 1897, and who by now had either gone "out" or were distributed over the country. A rocky road was cut right into and around the curve of the granite mountain that led from the Klondike ferry to Dawson. At midnight I rode down the front street to the hotel after an absence of two months, with the consciousness that I had laboured patiently in the interval, and that future results seemed hopeful.

Chapter 12

AUTUMN OF 1899

"Good morning," I said to Billy Edwards, wharf-keeper for the Seattle and Yukon Transportation Company. "When did you get here? The last time I met you was in Frisco."

"Yes," he replied; "then I owned and ran a street car line in Petaluma. Now I'm paid 100 dollars a month and grub, and damned glad am I to get it."

"Been here long?"

"About three months."

"Why don't you go to the mines?"

"Because I have no money nor experience. Was busted when I landed." And he added with a sincere laugh: "I guess you haven't been down to Dawson for long."

"No," I replied – "near two months."

"Well, walk around town; you'll see several other fellows who were somebody in California laying around here. Milty Latham, Sam Pond, Charley Fairbanks, and lots of others, all up here to make their eternal fortune."

Latham's father had been Governor and United States senator from California; Pond's father, Mayor of San Francisco. I met all of them later. They had come in over the ice, leaving the coast with ample supplies; but horses died, dogs died, food gave out, and finally, after several months' travelling, they arrived at Dawson in the early spring, in a most forlorn condition. But they possessed money and courage, though little experience, and after resting went to the mines, made purchases, and worked the properties with more or less – generally less – success the ensuing fall and winter.

Dawson was full of men and women. To promenade Front Street on the river-front was like walking for a block or two in the Strand. The street was sewered, macadamized, and side-walked. Shops with full stocks and plateglass windows occupied the east side. The west side consisted of wharves fronting the river. Scores of handsome women sauntered up and down dressed in most appropriate costumes. But one could see from their overbright eyes and carmine cheeks that they had been late overnights. The number of modest and refined women was still scanty. Wives and daughters were coming slowly. Homes had to be provided, and the future of the husband fairly well assured, before he dared to send for his family. Besides, people outside had such odd notions, both of Klondikers and the way they lived, that it took love and persuasion combined to induce women to come to the Far North. These imaginary terrors were ultimately dispelled, and the next year Dawson supported two schools and three churches. Still, it was not so bad as the winter of 1898, when an entertainment had been given at which an effort was made to exclude the undesirables. One of the two papers in Dawson observed that, if this purpose was successfully accomplished, not enough would remain to form two quadrille sets, which, though a gross falsehood, and contemptible in its origin and author, nevertheless effected its malicious design in making us out worse than we were to the "outside." The sharpest stabs come from those we know.

The east river-bank was lined with steamboats. I counted eleven. They told me that one boat arrived and departed, on an average, daily. These steamers came from up and down the Yukon, from White Horse and St. Michaels. A boat would arrive with 900 tons of freight. In twenty-four hours she was unloaded and gone. Men were paid a dollar and a half per hour as stevedores, and not a moment's pause was made until she was emptied and away for another load. No time to lose in the short summer. They were making the voyage from St. Michaels in sixteen days. It was twenty-one days the year before.

I met Captain McGinley, of the *Leah*, which had just come up.

"How did you make it so much quicker with the same boat and boilers than last year, when I was with you?" I asked.

"We burn more wood, for one thing," he replied. "Then we were to a degree restricted in the number of cords. Now we are told to make speed."

"Still, you did that, after a fashion, last year, and it's the same river."

"But not the same pilots," he quickly added, "for we have dropped all the Indians. Our pilots now are brought here from the Mississippi River. They were engaged for three years under a contract, though we can only run five months in the year. These Mississippi pilots came in this spring, and already know the shoals, currents, and depth of water, better than the Indians who have done nothing else all their lives. The Indian slows down in 3 feet, waits, searches, and puts down poles; the white man puts on steam and ploughs right through the soft mud into deeper water. But good-bye. Hear you're getting rich; hope it's true. I must be at St. Michaels in seven days at most."

Five minutes later the *Leah* had turned in the stream, set her bow down the river, and, going twelve miles, disappeared round Moosehide.

The captain's story recalled the instance of the moccasins and the felt shoes. Indians always remain Indians; the whites advance, and therefore improve.

Back of First Street were Second and Third Avenues, with cross-streets. The marsh surrounding my warehouse was gone, the ground dry and firm. A street passed its portals, and several cabins, with a small two-storey hotel, were built hard by. There were some shops in the rear and side streets of artistic proportions, with plate-glass windows, intermixed with old dirty cabins that were "old" indeed in our nomenclature, for they were constructed at least two years previously.

Horses, horses everywhere, with drays and wagons. It was easy to see the dog was doomed. The wharves were piled with immense quantities of compressed hay brought from the "outside," and even vacant lots on the streets were occupied with packages of it weighing 100 pounds each. On the gentle upper slopes of the plain, formerly a stagnant marsh, but now dry, healthy ground, were new cabins dotted here and there. Busy carpenters plied hammer and saw, and, in a word, a town of lumber and glass was replacing one of tents and logs. It seemed strange indeed to call at a house, to find a carpet on the floor, a piano in the parlour, and the house itself possessing three rooms on the first-floor, besides a little storey overhead. I noticed, nevertheless, that all the partitions ran only to within 18 inches of the roof, and that the stove, though bright and nickel-plated, was yet of immense size and in the centre of the largest room.

In the evenings, the autumn of 1899 was very much like the autumn of 1898. Of course, everything had been rebuilt since the fire of last April, and on a larger and more enduring foundation. Still, the gambling-saloons, with their dancing-hall adjuncts, occupied the same relative places in Front Street, and the same crowd went in and out — better dressed, it was true, more white shirts and polished boots; and there was a steady, hardened look in the clear faces of many of the men that indicated the professional gambler. As was said to me, half of Dawson's permanent population lived in the night and slept in the day.

Two of the dance-halls had been transformed into semi-theatres, where singing, dancing, and short plays of one or two acts, were given. These were frequented only by men; not, perhaps, that the plays, at least — though several were local productions — were so improper, but the theatre entrance was in the rear of the saloons, with faro and roulette on both sides, and scores of men, spitting, smoking, swearing, drinking, and gambling. It was a gauntlet that no woman could run.

In the saloon proper, mingling in the crowd, were young and handsome women. They played faro and roulette standing shoulder to shoulder with men, with as much nonchalance as though they were on the heavy velvety carpets in the Casino at Monte Carlo. They kept the gold-dust-weigher, with his big bright brass scales, busy, for I noticed that, while a few men played with currency, the women all carried pokes ostentatiously held in their gloved hands. They went up to the tenuous bar, with its round brass rod extending from the street window to the door of the theatre. The mahogany counter shone with the smoothness of the polished wood. Long narrow mirrors filled and gilded the wall behind, reflecting bottles and bottles of all kinds of beverages. The ladies observed their appearance in the glass, swishing their long skirts and silken petticoats to give a more coquettish touch, while one turned round to say to a crowd of men, most of whom were doubtless strangers to her:

"Come up, boys, and have a drink with me. There's my poke," throwing a well-filled buckskin bag of gold-dust on the counter.

She was brilliantly handsome, with an admirable figure and a charming toilette. She was a Sacramento schoolgirl, who had drifted from California to Oregon, and thence to the Klondike, or rather to Dawson, for she never went up on the creeks: it was not necessary. She was the most distinguished woman in the town, and held high court with her admirers. It was said that she had paid off a 10,000 dollar mortgage on her mother's ranch near Sacramento, was belted with a 1,000 dollar nugget chain, and could clean up and leave with at least 50,000 dollars.

That night I watched her for an hour, and between roulette and the bar she must have squandered 1,000 dollars. She lost and paid with great coolness and assurance, and, I noticed, laid her wagers with a knowledge and aptitude for the game that far surpassed my ability. For the matter of that, in all the years I spent in the Klondike I never gambled a dollar at faro or roulette. I had no desire, and, besides, I really did not understand the methods well enough. Moreover, I had no intention to fritter away in Dawson anything I might make at the mines. I felt that there was a wider and more cultivated field, and that, were I sufficiently successful, I could leave with a full heart, and say with Monte Cristo, "The world is mine." One man lost 21,000 dollars in one night at faro, and 5,000 dollars more within a week. He paid, of course, but it crippled his means, injured his reputation, and weakened his nerve. The temptations were manifold those lovely autumn months of August and September, 1899. It was a most prosperous season. Gold was brought into town by horse-loads. Miners would tell each other, not how many dollars or ounces they had cleaned up, but the number of pounds. Oh those halcyon days! The steamers were loaded with luxuries: fresh oysters, *pâté de foie gras*, fresh oranges, peaches, apricots, and candy.

It was odd to see a stalwart miner, with flushed face coruscating with health, and eyes flashing with physical energy, sauntering down the street, going into every saloon, treating every one present, were they few or many, at half a dollar each, his coat pockets filled with apricots, oranges, and candy, all mixed up indiscriminately.

"Hello, Steve! take a drink. Come on, boys, all hands to the bar. Oh, I say! have an orange. Here, you take one too, George. They're bully good. Just down from Vancouver by the Sophia. Only 50 cents each – dirt cheap. I haven't tasted such candy since I was a boy. Here, bar-keep! here's my poke. Snatch, but don't steal."

The bar-keep did not steal, but he naturally gave the down-weight on the scales to his employers. That alone amounted, in the larger establishments, to 100 dollars every twenty-four hours.

Chapter 13

WINTER OF *1899*

The water froze on Bonanza September 22, 1899. There was but little snow as yet, but the weather had been colder for a fortnight. I had stopped night sluicing on the 1st. Between ten and eleven the sun's rays softened the film of ice in the creeks, and we could pump water and wash gravel without intermission until seven or eight in the evening, when it again froze. Still, that ten hours' sluicing kept forty men at work in the mine and environs, for we put the dirt through very fast. When beginning to sluice in the morning, the water ran very slow at first over the ice-glazed riffles, and we flushed the thin ice between them by hot water and steam from a hose attached to the pipe that carried steam from the boiler. It is very easy to lose gold-dust in mining when the water is cold and icy. It seems to part, so to speak, with its specific gravity. Dash a stream of water into sluice-boxes filled and filling with dirt, and the stronger the water-supply, the sooner is the gold disintegrated from the gravel, and the sooner it sinks down to the bottom between the longitudinal riffles. But for cold running water interspersed with fragments of ice it appears to possess an affinity, and glides over the riffles and out of the boxes like soap. Miners are always chary of sluicing in cold weather, and carefully pan the tailings to see if more is being lost than ordinarily, for under any circumstances, even with our present new and improved processes of washing gold-dust, a percentage is always lost. I have heard that in some of the rich Eldorado mines "laymen" earned as much as 20 dollars a day by sluicing the abandoned tailings; but, of course, the mines on that creek were nearly all exceptionally rich, and, besides, they were worked in 1897 and 1898, when people were more careless and improvident than now. I think in our own mines we may have lost, perhaps, 5 per cent., certainly not any more. However, that was quite enough, and I was for ever changing the grade of the boxes, the quantity of water, and the shape, thickness, and direction of the riffles. If, when panning, which I did several times daily, I found a grain or two more of dust in the tailings than I thought ought to be there, I would worry the foreman, sluice men, and tram men until something was changed – very often without any real benefit. Still, one had to keep trying. It is only by efforts and experiments, as well as experience, that one can advance.

After the "freeze-up" we discharged most of the force, and prepared for winter working. We took gravel out of the mine through the tunnels and their branches, as usual. It was then sent down the hill by the tramway, and piled in big mounds on the creek, to be washed in the spring when the thaw came, and the blessed water coursed once more from the mountains to the sea. This process required two handlings of the gravel on the creek: first, when taking it out, and, second, when sluicing in the spring.

Winter working is, naturally, more expensive than summer working. Everything costs more. There are delays, and the men cannot do so much nor such good work. Still, every ton of gravel taken out left that much less in the mine, and brought me that much nearer to the "outside"-

that much closer to London, Paris, and the Nile, besides my loved California. Therefore I employed thirty men all winter, and by spring had a couple of pyramids of dirt piled high up on the creek banks ready to be washed when water came. I called the two pyramids Cheops and Chephren. Though they were not so old nor enduring as their Egyptian namesakes, yet they enabled me later on to view their ancient prototypes with grateful satisfaction.

I remained at the mine until the middle of November, building a little chalet on the hillside near the tunnels for myself, and mess-houses, with kitchen at the base, for the men. I intended to employ 100 men next summer, and it was my duty to provide good and suitable quarters. Then I wanted a comfortable little chalet for myself and secretary, as near the actual workings as possible. I had found the old office on the creek both unsuitable and inconvenient, being too distant and too public. It was like living in the street. My secretary would be with me in the spring, coming in over the ice from San Francisco. I felt I could find good use for an active and intelligent assistant, with the increased responsibilities of the future.

I designed new drifts in the mine and started them. I contracted for 2,000 cords of wood at 20 dollars per cord, for next summer, all to be delivered at the mine and creek "before the snow was off the ground." For a team of horses that could haul two and a half cords of wood on a sleigh over ice trails could not bring a single cord by wagon from the same place in the slush and muck of spring and early summer. The wood was cut about five miles from camp in the mountains, to the eastward and on the confines of Adams Creek. Birch, spruce, and a little pine and cedar, comprised the forest trees, mostly of moderate dimensions.

There were also some cottonwood or poplar trees in this Alaskan forest. Wood-choppers abounded. The country was full of men seeking employment, for but a small proportion of mines were working this winter, and then with a reduced force. People were beginning to learn that the summer was better in every way for handling the mines, so those miners who had no winter's job went to town, purchased provisions, found a partner or two, and then encamped in the woods, cutting the wood fast and free. There was an ample demand, and a good man could earn 7 dollars a day of ten hours' hard, hard work, felling the trees and trimming and severing them into cord-wood of proper lengths. There was labour and pay at one thing or another for those who chose to work. It was a golden paradise for all but the idle, though the glass did descend to the fifties below zero.

I stayed in Dawson at the Hotel McDonald, a handsome, commodious, two-storey structure, with bed-chambers on the second-floor, bar, office, and dining-room beneath. The arrangements for heating were simple and admirable. At the head of the stairs in the hall was a large stove of an improved pattern, nice, new, and nickel-plated. Filled with dry birch, it was a most comforting companion on a cold day. From it radiated pipes up and down the two corridors, opening on to which were room doors. By leaving the transom always open and the door ajar when one retired, enough of warmth was conveyed from the heat-pipes passing by next the corridor roof to make the chambers quite habitable. Of course, in these rooms the heavy double windows of thick though clear glass were never opened from November to March inclusive. Carpets covered the rooms, hall, and corridors. The chambers were nicely furnished, and all in all it was quite cheerful and homelike.

I felt invigorated, lifted up and emancipated. Why, when I heard the simple melody of "Annie Laurie" echoing from the piano in Mrs. McDonald's apartment, it was as if I were once more within the circle of civilization.

Dawson was changed. From the winter of 1898, with its moccasins, single-roomed cabins, and tree-stumps in the streets, to the winter of 1899, with its neat felt shoes, well-appointed cottages of several rooms, and clear, straight streets, was a transformation.

It was quite as cold as the preceding winter, but it did not seem so. We were acclimatized. Our bodies and blood had assimilated themselves to the conditions existing, and these conditions conveyed the highest health and mental buoyancy. In place of shivering and shuddering by the fire, we went out in the open, formed tennis-courts on the smooth clear ice of the river, with skaters as players. We took dog-sleighs and raced up the Klondike for pleasure and for profit. It was quite the fashion for ladies to drive dog teams themselves five or six miles from town, racing out and in with them like the most approved dog-driver. They were clad in short dresses, felt shoes, and fur caps and mitts. No fur cloaks – nor, indeed, cloaks of any kind – were worn on these expeditions, though at times the thermometer was incredibly low. The women particularly, who had passed a winter in the country, were, if possible, more hardy and healthy than the men. They looked with gentle pity on those "cheechaka" women who had come in during the past summer and fall. These latter, at the commencement of winter, would venture into the streets only under necessity, clad in furs, and fixed up generally like an

Eskimo or a porcupine. I have seen a lady whose third winter this was, appear in the street with rosy cheeks, bright eyes, and laughing lips, her fur hood thrown back, and chat with friends as nonchalantly as if it were 40° above instead of 40° below.

Tom Chisholm never wore anything but an old Panama hat on his head summer and winter, and Captain Scarth never wore gloves nor mitts, and never had a finger frozen.

I had come to Dawson to enjoy a pleasant winter. I knew that my mines were good, and would be quite productive next summer. I was content with my coming to the country, and was resolved to have a good time. As I had lived at the mines all summer, I knew few women, and not many more men of the town. But gradually I made acquaintances, and after a while gave a dinner to a few of my new friends.

The restaurant was fairly good, especially on the question of prices. However, I had not much to choose from, for it was either this or nothing. It is true that there were other restaurants, but these had no large room for a dining-party, nor, in fact, could ladies go there with equanimity. We sent up the mountainside and brought down ferns – evergreen fernery – obtained by digging under the snow. We also had berry bushes, with red twigs and branches like mistletoe. A red-topped grass, which grew quite as luxuriantly as pampas-grass on the La Plata, made pleasant wall decorations. It was fully 5 feet long, and was gathered in heavy bunches. Our musicians, five in number, were in general harmony a little discordant, but individually their instruments could always be heard and distinguished. The melodies were simple, good old tunes. We preferred those we knew, and which we also thought they must or should know.

The *menu* is appended, and I do not think that it is so very bad for the time and the place:

MENU

Huîtres Baltimore.

POTAGE.

Consommé Impérial.

Sherry.

POISSON.

Klondike grayling. Alaskan colihans.

Sauterne.

SALADE.

Homard.

ENTRÉES.

Fois de volaille. Pâté poulet.

Claret.

HORS D'ŒUVRES.

RÔTI.

Bœuf.

Champagne.

GIBIER.

Ptarmigan aux champignons.

LÉGUMES.

Petits pois. Asperges.

Port.

DESSERT.

Omelette au rhum. Fromage Rochefort.

Fruits fraiches. Noix. Raisins.

Sherry

CAFÉ. LIQUEUR.

The frozen oysters were a veritable gift of the gods, and had just arrived by dog-sleighs over the ice from White Horse.

Both men and women were in evening dress. How some of the men managed to procure their costumes is another story. There was only one tailor in the town, and he confessed that he never had made a dress-coat. He had practised his profession usually "north of 53°." Besides, adventurers going to the Klondike to make their fortunes naturally left their good clothes at home. Even the officers stationed at Dawson that winter scarcely included the military dress-suit or civilian evening wear in their kit. But the women – sensible creatures – had shown their prudence by not leaving anything behind, and demanded of us men to dress "like gentlemen." Well, we did it.

Other dinners followed, and a little later St. Andrew's ball. There were more Scotsmen in Dawson that winter than all other British nationalities combined except the Canadians. Scots and Swedes have always predominated in these Northern regions. Everyone that could get the proper habiliments attended. The town was ransacked for materials to make dresses and coats of the proper hue and cut. Any woman who could cut and sew was employed either for herself or her friend, usually for both. Tailors sprang up like the men of Cadmus, and received preposterous sums for suits "made to order."

Dawson became suddenly a "society" city. Nothing but rubber boots, moccasins, and felt shoes, with accompaniments of flannel shirts and fur coats, had been in evidence since its foundation; but, lo! it was "in the air" that those who did not go to the ball were out of the pale, and not among the elect and select. The committee in charge found themselves, indeed, on the horns of a dilemma in selecting the ladies, for there were those who wanted to go, and there were those who wouldn't go if the others went.

Now, in Dawson lived half a dozen women whose position and reputation were unassailable. These quietly assembled and constituted themselves a Vigilance Committee. All applications for ball tickets by ladies had to be submitted to them, or they would not go. If they did not go – well, the heavens might not fall, but the ball would fail. They did censor those applications mercilessly. No Grand Chamberlain of a Queen's levee scrutinized names more closely and made more inquiries – searching, remorseless inquiries – than did this Council of Six; and, my heavens! how much they did know about everyone! Who told them, and how did they find out? Living quietly in their homes, seldom appearing in the streets, meeting only a few friends, these half a dozen women knew the history of every other woman in the town, past and present – indeed, apparently, the future also. It then transpired that Miss Larkin was a divorcée from Seattle; that Miss Bertrand had a husband and two children in San Francisco; that Mrs. Charles was not married to her husband; and that the husband of Miss Godchaux had come to Dawson from Ottawa in the fall, and she had bribed him to go away and leave her unmolested.

These were the names of women who held respectable positions in town, and were supposed to be as good as anyone else. The great number of unattached and wandering nymphs were never included in the proscription, for they were not on the list.

Nevertheless, when the fateful night came, the number of ladies present at the entertainment was largely over a hundred, and Dawson plumed itself on possessing, in spite of the sifting process, so many beautiful and unexceptionable goddesses.

Quickly thereafter came the dinner of the ex-cadets of the Canadian Military School, which was a most finished and charming affair. Speeches were made, toasts drunk with good wine and plenty of it, and the table, with officers in military dress, looked like a banquet at the Hôtel Cecil.

We were becoming quite metropolitan. Meanwhile the telegraph-wire was for ever breaking, the letter mail was exasperatingly slow and uncertain, and there was no newspaper mail. Some people went out over the ice, but very few came in, and, take it all in all, we were very nearly as completely isolated from the "outside" as in the preceding winter, despite the apparent progress in comfort and conveniences we had made. So we turned with energy to our local sports and pleasures, for we were, as we sometimes felt, banished from the world.

A Jesuit hospital during the years 1897 and 1898 had been the only public refuge for the sick miner on the Klondike. It incurred a large debt for these services to the sick and destitute, and the idea of a bazaar to aid the hospital was started. Quickly a meeting was held at the barracks, at which the proposition was discussed and accepted, and proper committees selected. Mrs. Captain Starnes was chosen as head of the women, and I of the men, who were to assist and manage. Mrs. Starnes was a vivacious, piquante little French-Canadian of the most attractive type. Quick, witty, and charming, she was also energetic and inventive. We called her "La Petite Caporal." The Captain, her husband, who was half English, as his name implies, was at the time second in command of the police, and acted as judge and magistrate in the trial of petty offences. His Draconian judgments were feared and respected. He kept drunkenness and fighting at a minimum. When the police had stated the cause of arrest, "What have you to say?" demanded the magistrate of the culprit.

"Well, you see, your worship, I was out with Fred Olsen, and we drank a little hootch, and next thing I know was Jim here" – pointing to the policeman – "rolling me out of the snow. It was the hootch, your worship – that hootch that they make in West Dawson – and I'll be damned if..."

"Sixty dollars fine or thirty days on the woodpile. Call the next case," thundered the Court.

Harry Munn was arrested once for the same offence, and brought before the same judge. Now, Harry and Starnes knew each other quite well; but on the bench the Captain was as brusque and unbending as Rhadamanthus. Besides, he had a very proper opinion of the Court's dignity. So when Harry appeared, in company with other back-sliders, before the morning Court, looking as if he had spent ten nights instead of one in the gaol, for, alas! Harry forgot Cambridge once in a while, the Court was displeased.

"You see, Captain," quoth Harry, not yet quite fully recovered.

"I am not Captain; I'm the magistrate here."

"Well, all right, Magistrate. You see, I was only sitting down on the side-walk, cooling my fevered brow, when this miscreant" – pointing to the arresting officer – "disturbed my dreams. It was an infamous outrage. I was not intoxicated no more than I am now, and I denounce him before this august tribunal."

Just then the Court observed that Harry's hands were plunged in his trousers pockets. This was a most heinous breach of decorum.

"Where are your hands, sir?" said the judge in measured tones.

"Why, on my arms," replied the prisoner.

"Where are your hands?" again demanded the Court in deadly quiet accents.

"Why, where the devil should they be but here in my pockets," asseverated poor Harry, all unconscious of his crime, but never removing them.

The Court rose.

"Yes, in your pockets, where they should not be while being examined in open session. I have warned you twice. Officer, take this man to the gaol, and put him in solitary confinement for twenty-four hours. Let no one see him."

Harry was hustled off, not quite fully understanding how or why, and it took the combined influences of half a dozen leading men, including Starnes' superior officer, to permit the culprit to be seen. But he had to stay the twenty-four hours.

But I have wandered from the bazaar. There was but one suitable hall, controlled by Charley Meadows. Charley had a history – like some of the Dawson ladies. He had lived in Colorado, Mexico, and all over the West, had fought with Indians, and enjoyed the distinction of having been an Arizona Sheriff. Tall, lithe, erect, with long black hair and sparkling eyes, he was a typical Buffalo Bill, and shot and rode just as well as his prototype.

In August, 1897, Charley wandered into Dawson, accompanied by an itinerant scribbler. It was the winter when the richness of the mines was proven, but their extent was yet unknown. However, people not merely hoped, but expected that they would last for years, and millionaires were blossoming on every creek and in every saloon. Charley and his friend, Virgin, suggested to the gentlemen the idea of publishing a Klondike Gazette, containing the history of the country, and incidentally an epitome of these Klondike millionaires' careers. There was an immediate assent, and a month later the two friends left in mid-winter over the ice with 40,000 dollars.

The Klondike Gazette was to be published in San Francisco, and accordingly Charley engaged half a dozen elegant rooms at the Baldwin Hotel, one of its principal caravansaries. Between bottles he managed, at the end of some months, to print a document embellished with horrible portraits of the millionaires, and adorned with a "History of their Lives," and nothing more. Copies were given to whosoever would read, and the whole country laughed at the effusion.

Charley returned the following summer. Virgin didn't; he knew better. Charley's reception was – well, it was not wholesome. They threatened all manner of things, and if it had been an American instead of a Canadian town, shooting would have occurred. But the Canadians discourage that pastime. They actually put people into prison for shooting at each other in public. So nothing happened. After all, Charley was not to blame. He played openly on their vanity and ignorance, and did nothing criminal. But he was shunned. After a while he became associated with some theatrical people, and managed the theatre. It was vacant for this Christmas week, and so he let it for the bazaar, the only appropriate room we could find. The bazaar was opened with due approval. I delivered the inaugural address, and we had violin and piano duets, solos, choruses, tableaux, and dancing every night. Sixty-five women who had sewed and crocheted for weeks sold their fancy articles at small tables, and at fearful prices, to the good-natured miners. When half-past eleven arrived the bazaar tables were cleared away, leaving the hall vacant, and until one o'clock men could dance with ladies for a dollar a dance. The regular dancing and gambling halls were at a discount for that week.

The ladies of the bazaar wished, if it were possible, to see some dancing and singing by the actresses of these dancing-halls. Of course, they could not visit the Dawson theatres, and so had been deprived of this enjoyment. The suggestion was made to the vaudeville artistes, and they responded with joy. The forlorn girls were only too happy to be in the same apartment with decent women, and enact decent parts once more.

We had only to choose and reject. There was a girl, a contortionist, who was said to be quite too very bad, and after she was billed for Thursday night she received a message that her services would not be accepted. The poor creature wept and wept. She felt that she was indeed and for ever lost and ostracized, and begged to be permitted the privilege of appearing before the bazaar closed, threatening to commit suicide. With the consent of Mrs. Starnes, I allowed her to perform her evolutions on the last night, and it is pleasant to record that the ladies of the bazaar extended to her the most cordial acclaim, and later received the girl on the floor and kept her with them until the close. She had a charming face and figure, and finally wedded a wealthy miner.

The bazaar yielded for the week 12,000 dollars net for charity, and in addition brought people together, forming fond friendships that still exist.

On February 22 the Americans gave a dinner (at which the author of this book presided) to the Britishers, each American exercising his privilege to invite a Britisher guest. We were fifty at table, and music was furnished by the barracks band. Britishers and Americans alike supplied the mental condiments, and we parted with flags, bottles, and ourselves a little mixed, but still able to warble "Auld Lang Syne" at the finish.

Chapter 14

GALENA CREEK

Just before the first snow of 1899 Arthur Wellman and Jim Gild were chatting in the Aurora. Wellman was from Sydney, and Gild had drifted from Nova Scotia.

"When did you come in from the 'outside'?" said Arthur, as he poured the soda from a siphon on top of the Scotch.

"Last June; I came down in a raft by way of Chilkoot and Bennett. We had a lot of stuff, and made some money in selling. I've prospected all summer. Didn't want to work for wages, but now I'm nearly broke. And you?" Jim continued.

"I came in from Frisco by way of St. Michaels," said Arthur, "about a month ago. I've been over the mines some, but haven't done nothing yet. I don't like to hire out for wages, either. It seems to me that a man ought to do better'n that here in the Klondike."

"Then, you're looking for a lay," said Jim confidentially.

"Yes," answered Arthur.

"Then, Arthur, I'll tell you something on the quiet. Eh!"

"That goes, Jim."

"All right. Here it is. I know some Swedes who bought an outfit at the A. C. yesterday and went away to-day. They're gone to Galena Creek."

"Where on earth's that? Never heard of it before," exclaimed Arthur.

"Well, I'll tell you. You know Monte Cristo Island, about four miles up on the Yukon?"

"The one covered with cottonwood-trees?"

"Yes."

"Oh, I know it well. Some pals of mine are cutting wood there now for the steamers."

"That's good. Right opposite, on the other side of the river, is Galena Creek. It's not very long, and we can easily find the Swedes. They must have some reason to camp there. Let's go in shucks, buy a cheap outfit, and follow them. Maybe we'll strike it rich. It's a new creek, and not much explored."

"I don't know," said Arthur doubtfully. "I don't much like those new creeks. Seems to me, that if there was something there it would have been found long ago."

"But what are you going to do this winter?" said Jim.

"That's just it. I don't know," said Arthur. "It seems to me that before working for wages I'd rather light out again for Sydney. I can work for wages anywhere. Tell you what I'll do," he added, turning to face Jim. "I'll go in with you on this thing, but with this agreement: If we don't find anything by Christmas you'll buy my share of the grub and let me go, and I'll leave for the 'outside' over the ice."

"That's a bargain," assented Jim. "Let's go right down to the A. C. and order our stuff. We can get a canoe somewhere and start up the river tomorrow. I want to get right to work."

The very next day they were indeed up the Yukon near the shore, in a heavy boat loaded with supplies of all kinds excepting fresh meat. These partnerships were very quickly made, and loyally kept, without a written line or witnesses. Men trusted each other, and rightly, for there were very few evasions.

Gild and Wellman met the Swedes about a mile back from the river on Galena. Nels Johanssen knew Jim, and told him at once they had found some colours in a hole sunk the week before, but water drove them out when down only 8 feet, and before reaching bedrock.

"I don't know nothing more," said honest, stalwart Nels, "but me tinks it was some good. Mebbe not. Me don't give you no advice, that's all. Everyone says dam poor creek!"

And he turned with his axe to a half-severed birch. The two Britishers, though disappointed – for they had hoped Johanssen could tell them something more definite and encouraging – yet continued up the glen, and finally camped about four miles from the Yukon. At that point the creek-bed was narrow, and if there was gold it should be found on the bedrock. Shafts could not be sunk until winter, but in the weeks following they laboured hard and long, for there was the cabin to build, with bunks, table, and chairs; wood to cut for cooking and thawing, the tools and provisions to be brought up from the canoe, and the gravel cleared. The supplies were carried on their backs, for they had no dogs.

Finally, towards the end of October, after everything was snug and finished, the weather was cold enough to begin to sink.

"I hope we'll find a prospect," said Arthur, as he lighted the first fire.

"We've worked hard enough," said Jim. "I wonder how the Swedes are doing."

"Let's see: it's now two months since we came, and we haven't met a single person," mused Arthur. "I'd like to go down and see them, but this snow is too deep."

"And I'd like some fresh meat," said Jim. "I don't know, but I don't feel jest right. Let's take a day off, and try for a moose or a caribou. There must be some around here."

"Oh, no, no; let's get down to bedrock first, and see if we've got anything," said Wellman, who was impatient to know.

So the Swedes, the moose, and the caribou, were left unmolested, whilst the two men worked steadily on, the one at the windlass, and the other below in the shaft. Day after day they toiled, living sparingly on bacon, pork, beans, and floured bread. When the outfit was purchased, canned fresh meats and vegetables were very dear in Dawson, so they had bought very little of these invaluable articles of food, intending to lay in a full supply when they "struck it." The gravel was difficult to work, as it crumbled, so it was necessary to timber. The ground was deeper than expected, and the shaft was sunk 44 feet before the bedrock was found. That in itself was a bad sign, for the deeper the gravel the less likelihood of gold – a Klondike axiom. But they persevered with brave hearts, though Jim Gild felt more and more clearly that there was something wrong with him. His legs were heavy, his eyes were dull, and his arms refused to turn the windlass; so he exchanged with Arthur and went down in the shaft.

Still, his appetite was good, his brain active, and he thought little of these physical indications while digging down deeper to the wished-for bedrock. Two days after Christmas it was unearthed. It did not look well to the eye of a miner, for it was hard and flat and solid. Bedrock carrying gold lies at an angle, and the rock is brittle, breaking easily when struck by a hammer or pickaxe. Not a trace of gold could be washed out, though they dug down into the bedrock a couple of feet, and along its surface for quite a distance. The following Sunday Wellman went down to see the Swedes while Gild remained in the cabin. He was ill, tired, and despondent.

Arthur returned that night late, for the snow was deep, and he had to break trail. His face was blank, and he sat down heavily without saying a word.

"Ah!" said Jim anxiously, "I'll bet they have no better luck than us."

"Worse than that," said Arthur.

"Worse?"

"Yes – worse or better, as you choose. They've gone."

"What, left altogether?"

"Yes; shafts filled up, cache burned for wood, everything gone. I could hardly find the cabin. They sunk four shafts, while we've only sunk one. I guess this creek's no good, Jim, and we've about lost our time and grub."

The men sat there in silence, drawing nearer to the comfortable stove and thinking. There were no repinings nor reproaches, for these are the chances of the Klondike. But Jim was sick – more ill than he or Arthur knew. Presently the latter said:

"You know our arrangement, Jim: if we didn't find something by Christmas, that I would go out."

"Yes, I remember, and it's all right."

"Well, let's look over the grub after supper," said Arthur. "I guess you won't have to pay me very much."

"Not more than a dozen ounces," said Jim, with a grim laugh.

For there was but little left, and an ounce and a half from Jim's little bag settled for Arthur's interest in everything. The next morning Jim said:

"Cut me some wood, won't you, Arthur, before you leave. I don't feel very strong."

"Why don't you go to Dawson with me, then, and leave this damned hole?" exclaimed Arthur. "No well man should be alone in the Klondike, let alone a sick one."

"I'm too tired to go to-day, that's a fact," replied Gild. "Besides, I've but little money, and it costs to live in Dawson. I'll stay here a couple of weeks or so until the grub has gone, and then when I'm better I'll go up the creeks and try to get work."

Arthur could not persuade Jim otherwise, so he cut down several fir and birch trees, chopped them up to the proper size for the stove, and carried a big pile inside the cabin. The rest he threw just outside the door, where it could be gathered almost without leaving the hut, bade Jim a hearty good-bye, and that same night after supper left for Dawson. The distance was only a dozen miles, and after he came to the Yukon he struck the well-travelled trail from White Horse to Dawson. That Christmas week of 1899 was remarkable for the luminous splendours of the aurora, which, like the sun, blinded the stars with its brilliancy, and lighted up the snowy slopes of the bleak mountains like a silver chandelier in the sky. But a nightly recurring aurora indicated intense cold. The Indians never stirred when the Northern Lights ruled in the heavens.

Poor sick Jim knew this the morning after Wellman had left. When there are two men in a cabin, one or the other keeps the fire from being entirely extinguished; but Jim was sick and feeble, and nearly froze before he could make a blaze in the frost-surrounded stove. All day he cowered by the fire with just enough strength to warm and eat a few beans and a little bacon. His weakened legs could hardly carry his form to the bunk, where he crawled into the sleeping-bag. The fire expired that night for lack of fuel, and the next morning he could not leave the bunk. His gums began to ache and swell, his legs pained him excessively, and like a flash came the knowledge that it was scurvy. No wonder; he had eaten no fresh meat for nearly four months – nothing but old, almost rancid salt food.

The third day he felt he must make an effort or die. Crawling out of the sleeping-bag, he fell on the floor and became unconscious. He could not have lain there more than a few minutes, otherwise he would have been stiff and dead as a rotten log; but, in those five minutes before he recovered, his hands and feet were frozen. After regaining his senses he pulled himself into the bunk, and got into his sleeping-bag again in some marvelous way. There he lay for thirty days. Above him, on a shelf in reach of his hands, was a bag of lump sugar. By it was a sack containing a little flour, and on the table near the bunk was a candle, a few matches, and a tin coffee-cup. He gathered frost from the wall and the shelf with his frozen hands. There was an ample, daily-increasing supply of this food, and with the cup and candle he melted it into water. He immersed flour in this tepid fluid and devoured the mixture, sucking as dessert a lump of sugar.

For thirty days Jim Gild lived or existed thus, waiting, while the snow and ice buried the cabin deeper and deeper, and the tomb became colder and colder. He never lost consciousness for one moment, except when blessed sleep favoured him, though the scurvy-tainted gums covered his sound teeth until these began to drop out in his mouth whilst eating the moistened flour. He knew that no one had lived on Galena but himself, Wellman, and the Swedes, and they were all gone. He knew, also, that it was off the line of travel to Dawson from every point, and yet he breathed, hoped, and waited. Day after day he patiently reached up to where a calendar hung on the wall, and crossed off the days and weeks. On the last day of January, 1900, he marked the thirtieth day of his living death. He was cold, and his body was numb and motionless from the feet to the heart. He was like the petrified semblance of a man. His cabin was covered from sight by snow and ice, and the gloom of his sepulchre was terrible. It was difficult to imagine a more desperate condition, and yet he was rescued – only, indeed, to die a little later in Dawson.

Joseph Fox, with three others who were camped on the Yukon, came up Galena Creek this day, hunting for moose, of which they saw signs in the snow. Noticing in the desolate glen some blazed trees, a language that every prospector comprehends, they followed the signs until they nearly fell through the roof of the cabin. Even the stovepipe above the roof was completely covered and invisible. They broke in at once and found poor Jim Gild frozen, immovable, and all but dead in his sleeping-bag. The brave fellows built a fire and gave him a little tea and soup. Then two of the party returned to their camp, got a sled, and broke trail with it for five miles back to Jim Gild's lonely hut. He was placed on the sled and carefully, tenderly drawn by these men to their comfortable tent. The next day he was transported to Dawson and placed in the hospital.

When he left Dawson five months previously he weighed 150 pounds; when he returned he weighed 75 pounds. While in hospital, he said that it was not the flour, but the sugar, which had kept him alive so long, and that without the latter he would have succumbed in a fortnight.

Poor Gild's toes and fingers were amputated, but skilled and kind nursing could not prevail against his dreadful sufferings, and two weeks later he died, and was buried in the frozen ground of the cemetery, where he sleeps with many another unknown who staked his life in the Klondike venture – and lost.

Chapter 15

THE YEAR 1900

The winter changed into spring; letters arrived, and even an occasional newspaper was met with. The telegraph-line behaved better, and occasionally we read an item in the Dawson daily press dated London the day previous. I walked to the mine every few days during the winter to note how my two pyramids of pay-dirt increased in bulk. It was only thirteen miles, which were easily passed in three hours over the smooth icy trail.

The first days of April marked a new era. The temperature had sensibly moderated. Why, it began to snow again, which meant only 5° or 10° below freezing-point! It seemed actually warm. People discarded furs for sweaters. Every miner, owner, and labourer left for the creeks. Sluice-boxes were made, water-dams constructed, flumes built. The sun was up for sixteen hours, and we stayed up with it and after it. For in these mild days a man could do twice as much work as in the cold winter's twilight atmosphere. I left the imperial city of Dawson, with its diversified amusements and temptations, for Cheechaka Hill on April 10, and did not return even for a visit until June 1. A week after my coming the divine water began to percolate through icy crevices under snow-covered trees and bushes, in tiny rivulets which, uniting, formed a small stream gliding over the still thick but softening ice of Bonanza Creek.

Dave Jones, our foreman, a thorough Welsh miner, was an example of amazing activity and energy. He had visited Dawson but once all the winter during the bazaar. Though no longer young, he was as robust as an Olympian athlete. It seemed to me that he never slept. All hours of the night and day he was running up and down the hill, which was steep enough to make one pause and reflect. Every day, every hour, the volume of water in the creek augmented, and was watched with eager and gloating eyes. Though the snow was on the hills and the ice in the valley, yet we worked in shirt-sleeves. Our pure blood, clarified through the Arctic winter, leaped in the light of the sun, and we revelled in the joy of lusty life. Birds, too, appeared. We had seen none in the winter except those monstrous ghostly ravens that, in the dim fog always surrounding them, reminded one for ever of Poe's monody. But now came gentle spring birds, thrushes and redbreasts, which chirped and twittered in the trees and hopped boldly on the window-sill and into the open dining-room. Hill-crests, from which the sun had removed the white quilts, rose up covered with bracken and furze. The trees, while shedding their winter garments of snow, seemed to loom up more stately than before, and absorb the warm sunshine into their stiffened fibres. The miners scattered like mosquitoes over the country, already sleeping on the land slopes in their little tents with the fast-fading snow around, and deserting the stuffy cabins, where they had existed all winter like emigrants on a steerage ship.

I always reposed with the door ajar, so as to be easily called if required, and early, very early, one morning Dave rushed into my room like a couple of bears.

"For heaven's sake, what's the matter, Dave?" I said.

"Get up! Look!" and he threw open the door, through which I rushed in pyjamas and bare feet.

"What do you think of that?" said the good fellow, pointing in triumph to a large volume of water rushing down the creek, carrying ice, snow, and masses of dirt on its turbid current.

"It's come," he said, "in a heap, like it always does. But we are ready, and in two hours we will be sluicing, and I'll bet a big red apple that we won't have to stop all summer."

I tumbled into my clothes and ran down the hill. Every one of the eighty men in our employ was there before me, chaffing each other and almost cheering, but meanwhile working, and working well. In a week 5,000 men were engaged on Eldorado and Bonanza, sluicing the winter dumps and making ready for the summer.

We worked two shifts of eleven hours each, leaving only two hours of the twenty-four for rest. That was a long spell, but the season was short and the men willing; they were extra paid for extra time, and I pressed every one with restless activity. I wanted to make a good hole in Cheechaka Hill before the summer was ended, as I intended to run over to Europe for the winter. That was an agreeable summer season. It rained very frequently, with happy results, for it kept up the water-supply. There can never be too much water in a mining district. The rain fell as in the tropics, fast and continuous for a couple of hours, and then cleared off with bright sunshine. No one sought cover, no one stopped work for the rain. They did not seem to mind it, it was so gentle and warm, with no wind. I suppose there must have been umbrellas in the Klondike, but I don't recall any; certainly I never saw one up the creeks.

Early in May the ice "went out." That is to say, the river in front of Dawson ran smooth, and the immense blanket of ice that had blocked its progress for 1,800 miles was broken and piling in tumultuous confusion into the Behring Sea. This was the day of the year, and thousands of dollars were wagered on the date, the hour, and the exact moment when the ice should commence to move.

Strange, that to-day nothing but ice can be seen in the river, to-morrow nothing but water. Nature makes its changes at times with revolutionary rapidity. Then came boats, passengers, letters, friends, and more adventurers – regiments of them. It was a new invasion of the Northland. They scattered over the creek like raindrops. Only, instead of trudging in mud, with 100 pounds of supplies strapped to their backs, they walked jauntily up the good Government roads, well dressed and cheerful. We "sourdoughs" gazed at the well-groomed new-comers with an emotion of pleasurable awe. We were glad to see them, yet we were glad we had come in before them. Our positions were allocated; but they had yet to find and maintain theirs.

During June occurred the robbery described in another place. After the untimely departure of my cook Louis, with as much of my property as he could carry, I had for my private cook Mrs. Cole, the mother of "Swift Water Bill," who had married two or three Klondike sisters, one succeeding the other, with due divorces between. He had achieved quite a reputation as "Swift," which extended even beyond the boundaries of the North-West. He was not a bad fellow, however, and if he made and squandered two or three fortunes in as many years, whose business was it? Every man has his own philosophy. Mrs. Cole was a fairly good cook, and, what was quite as interesting to me, she seldom left the chalet, and never went to the Forks, which had been the ultimate cause of her predecessor's undoing.

During the whole summer I visited Dawson but seldom. We had telephone connections and a good road, so that all provisions and mine requirements could be ordered and delivered in a day. It was like a glimpse of heaven in comparison with the harassing difficulties of the previous year. I was out all day and all evening without coat or waistcoat, hatless half the time, running down and up the hill, in and out of the tunnels and side-drifts, very often on hands and knees; or up to the crest of the hill, unloading and measuring trees with the limbs and ends cut off for fuel to the boilers. I learned to be a blacksmith, and could sharpen a pick with any of them; a carpenter, and more than once repaired the wooden driver; a timber-man, cutting the timbers to the required size outside, putting them on the car, pushing it 600 feet into the heart of the hill, and then helping to set them up against the fast-falling dirt from the thawing roof that more than once broke our sets and tilled the drifts and tunnels. I knew none of these labours when I went there, but I learned to do them all. So true it is that what man can do other men can do, sometimes even without the necessary preparation. And this Klondike air is oxygen and champagne combined.

On August 14, 1900, Lord and Lady Minto came to Dawson, via Skagway and White Horse. That is to say, the Governor-General of Canada and his consort visited the Klondike. Committees had been elected, funds subscribed, streets cleaned, arches erected, and everyone was to have a three days' holiday. Their Excellencies arrived in a boat decorated by flags, and after landing were escorted by a general procession to the barracks, where Major Wood, the

Commanding Officer, had prepared for their reception his official residence – naturally, the best in Dawson.

The people had built two arches in Front Street, adorned with ferns and flowers; the English and American flags intertwined together. It must be remembered that a good two-thirds of the population resident was American, and, of course, they had contributed at least proportionately to all expenses. Under these arches the cortege passed, and we made no doubt their Excellencies and retinue were properly astonished at our Arctic display of greenery and finery. Two or three days prior to their arrival, Fred Wade, the cleverest Canadian that was ever in the Klondike, accosted me at the Club.

Said he: "A committee was appointed, with Alex McDonald as chairman, to get together a few nuggets and some gold-dust as a souvenir to Lady Minto of her visit to the Klondike. Alex has done nothing, the committee has done the same; it looks as if the whole thing is to go by default. Now, won't you take it up, and see if something can be accomplished?"

"Remember I am an American," said I to Wade.

"Oh, never mind that! We are all gentlemen, and she is a lady. That is all need be said."

"You really ask me to take it up?" I continued.

"Yes," he said; "you would place us of the executive committee under obligations. I know that if you start it will be done all right."

"How much ought we to give her?"

"I should think about 1,000 dollars would be a pretty good souvenir."

"But how about the Countess?" I persisted. "In America sometimes they would prefer to decline. I'll tell you what I'll do," I finally added. "When Lord Minto arrives I will see him, and, if it be agreeable, I'll try what can be done."

Wade thanked me, and thus it rested.

Alex McDonald was a brawny and gigantic Nova Scotian, one of the very earliest pioneers, made taciturn by nature and by his lonely existence for years in the primeval forests of Alaska. He had numbers of supposedly good mines, and was reputed to be by far the richest man on the Klondike. Though deceived by many, he was loved by everyone. But he required a spur, and I well understood that nothing would be done if it were left for him to take the initiative.

That evening the Governor-General held a viceregal levee, at which I was presented. I took occasion to tell him of the suggestion, and to ask if it would be satisfactory to Her Excellency. He very promptly and naturally replied that he didn't have a doubt of it. In fact, he thought Her Excellency would be very much pleased. So the next morning I hunted up Alex, told him what had happened, and asked him to mount a horse and ride up the creeks with me, which he did at once. We galloped up Bonanza to Eldorado and explained our errand. Not a man or a company refused. All – British, Swede, and American – asked, "How much do you want us to give?" In more than one case the poke of dust and the separate poke of nuggets were emptied into separate pans on the table, and we were told to help ourselves. It was very grateful and refreshing to see the spontaneous generosity of these lonely Northland miners to a lady who had come so far to visit them in their cabin homes.

There were two Australians working a lay on Cheechaka Hill, near my own mines. I knew them well, and ran up the hill to their cabin, while Alex visited some of his friends below. They were eating supper. I told McLeod of our errand.

"What do you think would be about right?" he asked.

"I think an ounce from you boys would be about the proper thing," I answered.

He went to the coat that served as his pillow, took the poke from underneath – it might just as well have been on the table – and weighed out an ounce on the small scales. The poke was plethoric, and the gold-dust on the scales looked spare. He turned to his partner with a grimace. "Bramond, he must mean an ounce from each of us; don't you think so?" Bramond said, "Of course," and McLeod, deliberately and carefully to the last grain, neither more nor less, weighed out a second ounce. I protested, but "Here, take the couple of ounces and go," he said gruffly; but I could see, under his rough manner, both the man's and the Australian's loyalty to a woman and a lady, separated as he was by half the world from his own women-folk.

We could have gathered twice or thrice the amount we selected; but we took only a few of the choicest small lumps and some of the best fine dust. Before I left Dawson I had drawn and given to a jeweler a design for a golden box, in shape like the miner's bucket of the early days, hoisted by windlass, and still used in many places. It was oblong and sloping at the bottom. On one side in repousse was a miner, pick in hand; the next showed a replica of the golden bucket with windlass attached, as used in the mines. The third exhibited Dawson, with the noble Yukon rolling on grandly to the Northern seas, and the last side commemorated Lady Minto's advent to the Klondike.

Alex returned that midnight, but I remained at my chalet, and rode to Dawson next morning. There I encountered Colonel Donald McGregor. This gentleman was a good old soul, who made life generally obnoxious to others by being generally good to them. Fred Wade used to say that he was born to make others miserable, but then Mr. Wade must have been prejudiced.

The Colonel usually stood at street corners in Dawson, delivering philippics against the Government, and emphasizing with his cane on the sidewalks. He reminded one very much of a certain type of Southern gentleman "before the wah." The Colonel was chairman of some one of the numerous committees, and conceived that his duties included the handling of the nuggets – after they were collected. So he had posted down to the barracks, seen Lord Minto, and arranged to present Lady Minto, at five o'clock the next day, with a most lovely lot of lumps of gold contributed by the miners. In the meanwhile Mrs. Major Wood had instructed me for three o'clock the next day also. Lord Minto, thinking, of course, that there were to be two different gifts, arranged the hours accordingly. I met the McGregor, as I have stated, in the street, and he at once said:

"I am very glad you have got so many nuggets. I've made arrangements to present them tomorrow."

"You've made arrangements! What have you to do with it, pray?"

"Why, I'm chairman of Committee No. 1; that takes charge of everything."

"But I'm not on your committees, and have nothing to do with committees. I've done this at the request of Mr. Fred Wade."

I knew that name would not soothe the perturbation of the Colonel's mind.

"Why," he exclaimed, "Alex McDonald is chairman of the Miners' Committee, and he went up the creeks with you."

"That is true," I replied; "he went up with me, but he had done nothing, and wouldn't have done anything unless I had taken it in charge at the request of Mr. Wade. Moreover, all the nuggets and dust are in my possession, my dear Colonel."

Off he stalked to see Alex, and I went to dinner. The next day it rained heavily. The jeweler had completed the golden bucket. It was a lovely and finished bit of work. Going to the bank, I filled it brimming o'er with the choicest nuggets of the Klondike, spangling and sprinkling them with clear, sparkling fine gold-dust, until it seemed a little treasure-box from Paradise. Then we wrapped it in white velvet and, accompanied by Alex, whom I had captured from the Colonel, and a third mining friend, we proceeded to the barracks. I thought by taking a devious turn in the by-streets, after leaving the bank in the pouring rain, that I had outwitted the Colonel.

But my American-Indian tactics were not equal to his Highland astuteness. There he was waiting for us halfway to the barracks, cane in hand and storm upon his lofty forehead. It was on Alex, however, that he looked with reproach, and the former seemed – well, very guilty. I hurried on without stopping, and there was nothing to do but follow me, for I had the bucket.

Presently, at three o'clock, the whole lot of us were ushered – just a little bedraggled – into the reception-chamber occupied by their Excellencies and their entire retinue. I had thought it only just that Alex, as the oldest and most conspicuous, as well as most successful, miner in the Klondike, should make the presentation, so I handed him the precious box, after removing its white cerement.

Poor Alex, though he had had timely notice, got muddled. Lifting the golden bucket in one huge hand, he pushed it toward Lady Minto, saying almost inaudibly:

"Take it, take it, Mrs. Minto: it's only trash, to be sure – it's only trash; but take it, take it."

And she took it, holding it in both fair hands, and looking from one to the other with something like bewilderment upon her pleasant countenance. I did not know whether to laugh or weep. However, I did neither, but, feeling the whole affair would degenerate into a burlesque, addressed a few words to her myself, as one of the miners who appreciated and consecrated her visit. I told her that we had sweethearts and wives at home who were waiting and praying for us; that her coming recalled again and once again the memory of home associations; that her presence and reception proved that it was not so difficult a place to visit, nor were we of the Klondike quite such barbarians as the outside world might conceive from its remoteness. I begged her to preserve the golden souvenir as a memento from the miners to a woman who had come thousands of miles to see them, and I told her how freely and gladly the golden grains had been given. I added finally that in other places her welcome might have been more splendid and elaborate, but in no locality had she and Lord Minto been received with more real gladness and sincerity by all, and especially, if I might conclude with so saying, by the Americans. She thanked the committee, when I had finished, in a few gentle phrases.

Meanwhile the Colonel, who had entered willy-nilly with us, stood towering and glowering at the whole scene. He was over six feet, and he looked to me then about sixteen. The volcano did not explode however, and we left the presence without disaster or catastrophe.

What was to become of the five o'clock presentation, and where were the nuggets for that? The Colonel stalked moodily across the barracks yard, regardless both of the persistent rain and of Alex, who was explaining things. But I had a short talk with the Governor-General when we shook hands on the veranda, and he laughed heartily when he quite fully understood the situation.

"Then, these are all the nuggets Lady Minto will get?" he queried, with a smile.

"I'm afraid so," I replied.

"I hope she won't be too much disappointed," he continued, with a chuckle. "I'll send an orderly to tell the Colonel that I understand there has been a mistake, and that I know the offering at 5 P.M. will not take place."

He did so at once, and the Colonel's stern visage partially relaxed, while Alex looked relieved. Still, the Colonel disdained to note my presence when we parted at the first street corner, and I regret to write that I fear his anger is not even yet entirely dissipated.

The next day the viceregal party went up Bonanza in carriages, accompanied by a town retinue of sundry members of the committee and – Colonel McGregor. They lunched at one of the large mines, and made a visit to the interior of the tunnels and drifts. The method of mining, especially the thawing of the frozen ground, was new to the Governor-General, and he took great interest in watching the exact process of using steam points for thawing, which had come by that time into more general use, and had quite superseded the early and crude custom of wood-burning. In other ways, too, we had largely gained by new methods of extracting the gold.

The next day was spent in driving about Dawson, and in receiving complaints from miners and citizens who desired the laws amended. Though the Governor-General possessed no real executive power, yet the fact that he had made a personal visit to Dawson would render his observations and suggestions of great weight to the Cabinet at Ottawa, if he chose to make any. He was a cool, careful man, with infinite tact and savoir-faire, and, it seemed to me, must have fulfilled his sometimes onerous duties with justice and judgment. So the miners, both in committees and individually, made their numerous grievances known to His Excellency, who received all who applied, and made notes when documents were not presented.

It is quite true that no community is entirely content with the laws under which it is governed; and this is still more true when it has had no voice or hand in the framing of those laws. A number of ordinances had been promulgated by the Ottawa Cabinet for the government of the Yukon territory. Probably only a misty conception of the condition of affairs in the Klondike existed at Ottawa when these decrees were announced. Some were good, some were bad, but an especially obnoxious one was the royalty of 10 per cent. on the gross product of the mines, exacted direct from the miners. Apart from the excessive amount of the royalty, which in some cases almost amounted to confiscation, the miner complained of having to pay it exclusively.

The trader and merchant – Dawson or city men, as we miners called them – naturally sold goods at as large profits as possible, and were paid in gold-dust without deduction. But the miner who took out 10,000 dollars, at a cost in expenses of 9,000 dollars, had to pay the royalty of 1,000 dollars, leaving him nothing. This was manifestly unjust; for as gold was the sole product of the country exported, the tax should have been uniform, and distributed among all the holders and exporters of it, and not have fallen on the direct producer alone. This has since been remedied, and a moderate tax on gold exported only is now imposed.

Then the system of locating and measuring claims was immature and tentative. It was quite true that the Klondike presented new problems and questions not hitherto known, because of the character of the frozen ground. If the Government had sent in an experienced Commissioner when the first new questions arose, to examine and report what changes might be advisable, it would have been an excellent action.

Nevertheless, Lord Minto promised to lay all complaints before Sir Wilfred Laurier, and there was sent to the Klondike shortly following his departure a number of amended regulations, which were doubtless due to his benevolent action, and so credited to him by the residents of the district. The Governor-General and party left the same afternoon at 7 P.M. on the *Sybil*, and the *Klondike*, after its three days' happy holiday, returned to the usual avocations of gambling, drinking, and delving for gold.

In the middle of September we stopped sluicing – a week sooner than last September, but it was now freezing every morning, and I had exhausted a certain portion of the mines that I had laid out as my task for the year. So I left everything in charge of the foreman, and descended to Dawson, feeling that I was justified in taking a winter abroad. The city was thronged with miners in from the creeks, also "going outside."

At mid-day on October 3, 1900, the steamboat Canadian left Dawson for White Horse with 150 passengers, of whom I was one. Over twenty-six months of exile from the world, including two Arctic winters, had been added to the days that are past since I landed in the Klondike town. For that entire period, with all its vicissitudes in the way of food, comfort, and temperature, I had not been ill one day – scarce one hour.

Indeed, I was stronger, more active than before, and with buoyant spirits. I felt like one of the conquistadores sailing home from Peru to Spain.

There were others on the boat in a like mood, and we made a merry party. Some of them had been in the northern wilds since 1897, and, oh, how happy they were to be gliding towards civilization! It was not a boisterous, bawling happiness; these old pioneers were accustomed to experience sorrow and joy in silence and solitude. But one could see the perpetual smile, the clean, shrewd, bronzed faces, the clear eyes, and the readiness of everyone to talk with everyone else on any subject, and never disagree. Before the day was past we were all one happy family; but still, somehow, we only talked of Klondike hardships and successes or failures. For we were leaving with as much regret as pleasure, even if that be a paradox. While it had been banishment, yet it was a self-imposed one, and I think few of us passengers homeward-bound regretted this episode in our lives. Among the women was one from Melbourne, who had gone in three years before us with her brother. They had kept an hotel in Dawson, a road-house on Sulphur, a saw-mill on the Klondike, a store at Caribou on Dominion, and finally secured a good mine. She was going home to the old folks with a good little fortune, her rosy cheeks beaming with health and happiness. We were amused when she told us her history at the supper-table, for her numerous attempts at success before the right one was found had been the experience of most of her listeners.

During the afternoon I walked with the captain through the card-room. He was showing me the boat. I observed on one side of this room, upstairs, a number of wooden boxes about 3 feet long and 1 foot high, each bound by iron straps. They were piled together any way, and covered in part with a few empty flour sacks, old and dirty stockings, shoes, empty sardine and oyster cans.

"What are those boxes there for? Why don't you pitch them down below with the other freight?" I asked the captain.

He looked at me with an open smile on his wholesome face.

"You don't mean to say that you don't know what they are, and you've been in the Klondike three years?" he asked in answer to my question.

"I don't know," said I. "You see, I've been up to the mines most of the time, and don't know what you fellows do in Dawson and on the river."

"Well," he said, "it's only this: Each of those boxes is zinc-lined, and contains 300 pounds of gold-dust. We have no safe or vault on the steamboat, so we have to throw them in that corner."

I counted twenty-nine. Over 4 tons of gold-dust without a guard! Of course one could not run away very well on a river with a box containing 300 pounds of gold, yet the primitive simplicity of it all was charming. Ah! those were good old days.

The river narrowed, the water became clearer and the current less rapid, as we voyaged south. Hills encompassed us on both sides, with few or no trees. It was evidently a mineral or volcanic territory, and quite different from the densely wooded alluvial land north of Dawson.

In places on the high banks, where waters had cut a chasm down to the river-bed, could still be seen, like the segment of a fruit cake, the several strata which made the original deposits of gravel, asphalt, coal, pebbles and clay. Nature's laboratory exhibits its latest efforts in the Northern latitudes.

After steaming through Lake La Barge, from whence issue the head-waters of the Yukon, we traversed Fifty Mile River to White Horse. Fifty Mile is the clearest stream I ever saw. It is 100 yards wide and 10 feet deep, the bottom sprinkled with large boulders. Every grayling, every large stone and pebble, even the little pollywogs scampering about the bottom, were visible as in a kaleidoscope. The Canadian only drew 4 feet, and Captain Scammel enjoyed himself in a quiet manner, steering the vessel, to our amazement, right over some immense rock that seemed to be just below the water's surface. In four days from leaving Dawson we were at White Horse. The place is thus baptized because it is built just below the rapids on the short river leading from the Lakes to Fifty Mile and La Barge. The Indians gave these falls the picturesque name of White Horse, and one might say it is not inappropriate, looking on the surges of gray foam leaping and dashing over the sharp jagged rocks that formerly bridled them. But no White Horse, no Black Horse, could stop Klondikers from hastening on to the "outside." Just about half a dozen of us ran up to look at the falls, and then ran down again, for the train was ready. Think of it! A train, a special train, to take us to tide-water. Why we had almost forgotten what a locomotive resembled. We were in a delirium, and the sharp curves, the majestic depths, the towering cliffs, the narrow track where, at Danger Pass, the very cars over-hung the rushing snow torrent thousands of feet beneath, did not restore our faculties, until we saw unfolding, as we rushed down the cañon, the calm, obstructive sea. The 112 miles of railway, only finished this year, was crossed in five hours, and in summer it is a most attractive journey. It obviates all the physical difficulties that in years past made entrance to the Yukon basin so pregnant with trouble and hardships. Between Skagway and White Horse are included the precipitous mountains and difficult water-courses that made Chilkoot the Pass of Fear, and caused the loss of many lives. But that is all ended, and one can travel from Vancouver to Dawson with no more trouble and time than from Vancouver to Ottawa.

After a day in Skagway, where the fishing is good, the steamship Queen left with our people for Seattle, via Van-couver. In three days we were at the former place. The voy-age is delightful, with numerous islands on both sides, and recalls the Japanese Inland Sea; but the Alaskan islands are frozen, and intersected at points with blue-veined glaciers that live and throb for ever, adding to the ocean and level-ing the land. We passed a number of salmon canneries located on the islands, and immense numbers of the fish were being cut and canned, though it was about the end of the season.

At Seattle I made close connection by rail with San Francisco, and in forty-eight hours I was home, eleven days from Dawson, and nearly two years and a half after I had departed for the far, unknown North.

Chapter 16

THE ROBBERY

On July 4, 1900, I was due in Dawson to deliver an address. This was known to my cook, Louis Jacques. He had been engaged by me a couple of months before at a wage of 150 dollars monthly, as the best cook on the Klondike. In our little chalet on the hill there lived only my secretary and myself, so the duties of Louis were not onerous. He proved himself a true disciple of Vatel, and many an appetizing little entrée he made, at times out of slender materials. Faithful, courteous, prompt, and yet taciturn, quiet, and retiring, he delighted me, and made me think more than once that, even in the Klondike, there were gastronomical pleasures that might well be envied by those on the outside. We had salmon fresh from the river, grayling from the lakes, rabbit, ptarmigan, moose, caribou, bear, and partridges, besides fresh tame meats from the "outside."

On the night of June 30 I told George, my secretary, to go down the hill shortly before midnight, and stay there until after one o'clock. Our night-watchman was absent, and I never left the sluice-boxes unguarded, especially between twelve and one o'clock, the hour during which the water stopped while the men took their midnight meal.

In the meanwhile, dressed in pyjamas, I threw myself down on my narrow cot. It was a warm night, very clear, and I left the door of my office, which was also my bed-room, ajar.

At half-past ten the sun had declined below the horizon, leaving behind a thousand gorgeous hues, filling the sky as with a volcano's eruption. Nowhere are the colours clearer nor the afterglow more grandly impressive than in an Arc-tic sunset. Nearly up to midnight the whole heavens were ablaze with varied hues, and but slowly – very slowly – did the gray night chase them away.

An hour and a half after midnight George returned to the chalet. The rising sun was already indicating its rapid return by a subtle clearing of the atmosphere. He found Louis sitting in the kitchen fully dressed and reading.

"What are you doing so late?" said George.

"I'm sick," said Louis, "and have been taking some medicine."

"I see you have a pair of those new style red boots on. What did you pay for them in Dawson?" continued George.

"Twelve dollars," responded Louis, looking somewhat sullen, for George seemed inquisitive.

"Well, I'll go to bed," said George.

"Don't mind," said Louis, "if you hear me moving around, as I can't sleep."

George lay down on his bed in the room adjoining to mine, the two separated by a thin partition, not ascending to the log roof, and pierced by a doorway, over which hung a portiere. Still farther along the same floor was the kitchen, separated in like manner from George's chamber, which was also the dining-room; that is to say, the chalet, with its space of 16 by 30 feet, was divided into three rooms, marked by the two partitions, with portiere door-ways.

At 8.30 every morning Louis brought me a small cup of black coffee, and also carried in the tub, into which he emptied a couple of buckets of cold water for my daily bath. I was nearly always awake and waiting. But this morning Louis did not come, and my watch, lying on the small table by the cot, told me it was nine o'clock. So, after vainly calling, I arose and went through George's room to the kitchen. No Louis, nor was the fire started in the stove. I awoke George from a deep slumber, and said: "What's become of Louis?"

"I don't know," replied my secretary. "Oh yes! I remember now that he had not gone to bed when I came up last night, and said he was sick."

"Ah, then," I observed, "he must have gone to the Forks this morning to see a doctor. He might have told me so before going. He may not be back to-day. However, get up, George, and get me my bath. I must have that, though I can't have coffee."

While dressing after my bath, it presently occurred to me that now was a good time, while Louis was absent, to weigh a bag of gold-dust, and learn how Avoirdupois compared with Troy weights. All our gold was weighed in ounces, the market value of each ounce being 16 dollars. We cleaned the gold-dust from the sluice-boxes below on the creek every two or three days, and put the results in the safe, to which there was only one key, kept by George. This was sometimes a longish task, taking three or four hours, if the gold were mixed to any degree with black sand and pebbles. I never liked to open the safe except on "cleaning-up" days, and this Louis well knew, also that I should not clean up until that evening.

"George," I said, "open the safe and take out one of the full bags. Let's weigh it with the butcher's scales in the kitchen before Louis returns. This is a good chance while he is away."

The small safe was sunk in the corner of the dining-room, which, it will be remembered, was the second room, to a level with the floor, and fastened by inch-link chains to the solid beams that supported the floor beneath. These beams, a foot thick, lay upon the ground. He opened the safe while I was shaving with my back to him. I heard a sharp ejaculation, and quickly turned. George was looking down into the opened safe.

"How many bags of dust, filled and sealed, should be here?" he inquired.

"Two," I answered, "besides four more partially filled, and also the nuggets."

"There's only one full bag," he said in a frightened tone. "Come and see."

In two steps I was kneeling down by the safe. I always put the bags in myself, locked the safe, and gave him the key. After a moment's glance I turned to him, and said:

"A sealed bag, containing 400 ounces of fine dust, is missing."

We took out all the others – about 100 pounds weight including the nuggets – but they did not seem to have been disturbed. I examined the lock and keyhole, but there was no mark on the smooth nickel surface such as might appear from a violent opening. I did not suspect George, for whom I had sent to San Francisco the previous winter, as I knew he was entirely faithful; but he had the only key, and it was clear the lock had not been forced. We stood up and faced each other blankly.

"Tell me again about Louis," I finally said.

"Well, I told you all that a little while ago," he replied in a querulous tone.

No one is completely calm, no matter how innocent, when confronting possible accusations.

"It's strange," I continued, "that he went away without informing me when he might return. I wonder when and where he has gone."

"Oh yes, now I remember," said George eagerly. His face cleared. "Why, he had on his new heavy pair of boots at two o'clock when I came up from the sluice-boxes."

"What!" I exclaimed, "his new boots, and yet sick. Don't I remember to have seen you leave your key about on the table while cleaning the dust?"

"Yes, but I never leave the room until I am finished and the dust locked up. Last night, when I went to bed, I had it attached to a string around my neck."

"It's all clear to me," I said. "Louis has picked up that key while it was lying on the table, and made a model in some way. It was not difficult, for I know you have been careless. I've seen the key myself on the table and the gold scales when it should have been in your pocket. He has taken the largest bag of dust. He couldn't well take more, for that weighs 25 pounds, and he must have gone direct to Dawson on foot, thirteen miles. It proves, however, that he has no accomplices, which is a relief. I wouldn't like to think that any of the miners were with him. We shouldn't know whom to trust."

Poor George was radiant, but yet trembling, for I added:

"You must go up to the Forks and see the sergeant; Louis might be hiding around here. You'll have to tell him that you had the key, and the chances are he will ask you straight questions; but don't be afraid. It's Master Louis, and we'll get him."

There was a telephone at a miner's cabin 100 yards away, and I ran there, after locking the safe and putting the key in my pocket. I was soon in communication with the police authorities at Dawson. I told them of the robbery, and of my conviction that Louis had gone down the river. Forty miles from Dawson would bring him into American territory. It was a common and constant refuge of criminals escaping or banished from the Klondike. I offered to pay expenses if they would send a boat with a couple of officers after the fugitive. They promised to make immediate inquiries, and I returned to the chalet. Hardly had I left the telephone, when the man who kept the Klondike River ferry stepped into the barracks at Dawson, having come directly from his ferryboat, two miles distant. This is the statement he made:

Two men had arrived, spent with fatigue, at the ferry about five o'clock. One of them had a sealed bag of gold-dust, and carried it on his shoulder, enclosed in a flour sack. He bought a Peterborough canoe and provisions at a little grocery hard by, the purchases reaching about 150 dollars, which he paid by opening the sealed sack and asking the grocery-man to weigh out the sum due.

"Where did you get all of this dust?" the ferryman, who was present, said.

"I've been working for Senator Lynch as his private cook for almost a year at 150 dollars a month, and I had some money besides, so I bought the rest of this dust from him, as I am going 'outside,'" the man replied.

Now, the ferryman knew that I had been living in Dawson part of the preceding winter, and during that time had no cook or servant at my chalet; but he said nothing.

"Who is this man with you?" he presently asked.

"I picked him up on the road, and gave him 5 dollars to change with me in packing the dust. I'm going to give him an ounce more to help me row the Peterborough to Moose Creek below Dawson."

"Why don't you stop in Dawson?"

"Oh, I'm in a hurry to get to Nome, and there is no steamer at Dawson. I've got a partner at Nome who writes me to come at once. I had his letter only yesterday."

So Louis left with his convoy. The whole story seemed unreal to the ferryman. The bag evidently contained 6,000 or 7,000 dollars – too much for a miner or a cook to have gained by working for others in a year.

The police authorities possess special and unusual powers in the Klondike region, and those whose connivance at, or concealment of, crimes comes ultimately to the knowledge of the officers undergo suspicion, which would be inconvenient for many avocations. Therefore the ferryman hastened as soon as he could to the barracks.

With my telephonic communications and the ferryman's information the course was clear. In a couple of hours they found photographs of Louis in Dawson, and the man returning from Moose Hide was met on his entrance into Dawson, and interrogated by the police. He told them that Louis and himself had steered the boat down the Klondike to its junction with the Yukon, and gone down the Yukon – which is here half a mile wide – on the opposite side, away from the city front and wharves. At Moose

Hide, a couple of miles below, Louis returned to the east side, gave the man his ounce, and set him ashore.

One hour after mid-day saw two Canadian policemen start with a rush down the river. Louis had six hours' start, and the current was rapid, but the officers had the police racing canoe, and were trained rowers. There are no rapids nor other obstructions for hundreds of miles, and the broad, mighty river sweeps swiftly onward, noble and majestic, to find a grave in the Northern seas. The dark lines of fir and birch trees upon the banks are unbroken save by the tent of an occasional wanderer cutting wood for the river steamers. After passing Eagle, the river stretches away to the westward for 200 miles, unmolested by a single hamlet, bounded by granite hills that rise sheer up in line, like battlemented walls overlooking the deep waters that foam against the perpendicular base. All night long the police canoe raced down the river ten miles an hour. There were no stops. It was light enough all through the hours, and one slept while the other kept the boat where the waters ran swift and deep. They ate while voyaging.

At ten next morning, when they had traversed 200 miles, a boat was descried on a sandy spit. The officers softly landed by its side. A moment's observation told them that the man soundly sleeping in the canoe was Louis. There was no mistaking his face, and, besides, he had a rifle and pistol, weapons that no honest man found necessary in the Klondike. They consulted. This was American territory. They had no right nor authority to arrest him, as they were British officials. They had hardly expected to overtake him, except in some place where American officers of the law would be present, but they had gone fast and far, and Louis was exhausted with his vigils and labours.

When Louis awoke from a dream of rest he saw, as he sat up, two men coolly frying some meat over a little fire built between a couple of stones. He was nervous and terrified, and much denser men than the shrewd Klondike detectives would have noticed his agitated appearance; but they greeted him cordially, said they were prospectors going to Nome, and invited him to eat with them. They asked no questions, but he said that he was going to Circle City, the next town, about 100 miles below. After breakfast he left, anxious to get as far from Dawson as possible. They slept and rested a few hours, and then leisurely started, confident of overtaking the thief when they chose. The lovely Arctic July day declined farther towards the horizon, the sun still brilliantly shining in the clear heavens. Birds carolled lightly amid the shore trees, and salmon scales glittered in the sunshine as the fish, on their way up to the lakes, leaped above the flowing waters. The raven watched diligently on tree branches over the water, for many salmon were stranded in the shallows, flung there by the impatient army of their fellows racing up the stream. Far away and above glided through the windless air the Arctic hawks, resembling bald eagles, sweeping the horizon in rapid circles. A silver fox with its shining coat turned from the river as the boat swept round a curve, and was gone like a meteor in the bushes, leaving neither sound nor motion to indicate its presence.

On through the night hours went McIntyre and Judson, the light canoe with its smooth keel making no more noise in the water than the fox in the glen. Towards morning two boats were ahead. One was Louis's. The officers took the paddles out of the water and let their boat drift. Meanwhile Louis in his mad flight with the stolen gold had overtaken a canoe with a solitary occupant. This man was named Henry, and had been ordered out of Dawson by the authorities. There were many people of both sexes, gamblers and others, who lived like vultures on the miners when these latter came to town from the creeks. Very often some of these people became specially obnoxious, and the police then gave the option, "Down the river or the wood-pile!" The former alternative, of course, was chosen, so down the river they went to Forty Mile, Eagle, or Circle City, where they formed a class of the expatriated. It was one of these gentry that Louis had met, and with whom he was paddling along, conversing while their two boats floated downward with the current, side by side.

Henry knew all the police of Dawson. He had had an intimate acquaintance with them, and recognised McIntyre and Judson while they were yet far in the rear. He had also observed Louis's haggard air, and yet he knew that he was not one of the "rounders" of Dawson. Something must be amiss, thought this shrewd scoundrel to himself.

"Well, pard," he said to Louis, "whose cook did you say you were?"

"Senator Lynch's?"

"Where?"

"On Cheechaka Hill, near Bonanza. He has a rich mine there."

"Oh yes, I know of him. Why did you leave?"

"I got tired, and want to see Nome."

"Anything wrong with you and the Senator?"

"No. Why do you ask?" said Louis in a startled tone.

"Oh, nothing, except those two men behind are damned Dawson policemen, and they are after someone. It isn't you, pard, is it?"

Louis collapsed. It was his first crime, and fear and fatigue had quite unmanned him.

Just then the police boat passed them, Henry hailing the policemen, who replied shortly, for they regretted the recognition. As their canoe glided ahead, Henry said to Louis:

"Do you remember the name of the police boat?"

"No."

"Why, everyone knows it is called the Victoria. Just look under the stern of the boat ahead, partially covered with the tarpaulin. McIntyre had it covered since leaving Dawson, I suppose, but the tarpaulin got loose when they left camp after you."

The word Victoria, still half concealed, was visible, sure enough, and it left no doubt in the guilty conscience of Louis. In abject trepidation, he confessed to Henry.

The latter worthy was buoyant. "Now I see it all," he said, when Louis had concluded. "The rascals are going ahead to Circle, to get a warrant, and wait for you. But I can save you."

"How?" cried Louis.

"It will cost 500 dollars," replied the careful man of affairs, "and the dust at once, or I leave you."

"Take it – help yourself; but, for God's sake, don't leave me in the lurch!" said the miserable thief.

Henry cut the heavy bag of gold-dust from the flour sack in which it was wrapped at the bottom of the canoe, and then opened the gold-dust bag itself. He filled two tobacco-pouches with the glittering metal, taking 1,200 dollars, as was later ascertained. These he carefully hid in his shoulder sack. Then he poured the rest of the dust into several smaller bags that Louis and himself found in their belongings, and returned them to Louis. This done, he cut my bag into strips, bound the strips around the iron rowlock, and dropped it down into 40 feet of water. The bag had been sealed with an Egyptian seal, and the mark could not have been removed. That evidence was for ever gone.

Louis looked on in silence, while the two canoes floated together tranquilly down the limpid stream. When he had completed these acts, Henry said to Louis, in a deliberate voice:

"In front of Circle City is a large island extending several miles. The current takes one on the left to the shores of Circle City, where the officers will be waiting for you, but there is another channel on the right or northern side of the island. Everyone don't know this last channel, nor how to go through it; but I do. I was there last year, while staying in Circle, so I'll guide you through while Mr. Policemen are waiting, and before they find out you will be a couple of hundred miles below Circle on the way to Nome."

Louis was content and glad. He thanked his saviour most volubly, and made no comment on the two tobacco-pouches, though he well knew that a single one held more than the agreed amount. Thieves, by some law of compensation, cannot keep all stealings. There be other thieves stronger or warier who take from the first. Now, Henry, having his reward on his back for services not rendered, had no intention of performing them. He had no wish to go to Nome. He had started for Circle, and to Circle he would go. He had friends there who awaited his enforced coming from Dawson, and he could now meet his girl, whom he had sent on by steamer, with full pockets. Up in these regions people are more or less callous to the wrongs or sufferings of others. A quiet though intense selfishness is engendered by the feeling of being so remote and solitary. Not that it rises to the extent of doing wilful injury, only to a careful regard for one's own, and a careless regard for that of others. So when Henry steered to the sandy beach of Circle City, and quietly sauntered to the nearest saloon, leaving the slumbering Louis to be awoke and arrested the next minute by the Canadian officers, who had obtained the necessary warrant, he felt none the worse for springing the trap.

The denizens of Circle were in part a scurvy lot. Outlaws from Dawson, and yet fearful to descend the river to Nome, where they would meet civilization after a fashion, they poised at Circle like vultures, watching for the canoe of the "expelled" or the miner. The array of whisky-shops thronged with women on the water street invited entrance. Nay, they forced their attention on the traveller. Toll must be paid, or truculence and fighting would follow. Poor Henry was robbed as completely as he had robbed Louis.

In two days wine, women, and cards had taken from him his 1,200 dollars, leaving him again without a cent, and on the third day he shouldered a pick and shovel, together with some food, and started on foot for the mines of Mastodon Creek, 100 miles' fearful tramp over marshes, jungle of brush and trees, with mosquitoes and mountains thrown in.

As for my good missing cook, Sergeant McIntyre found an embarrassing condition of affairs. Though the United States marshal had given him an arrest warrant, there was no gaol. McIntyre employed four enterprising American citizens to guard the prisoner in a mouldering cabin, two by night and two by day, for 5 dollars each per diem and keep, which meant 2 dollars more. What remained of my gold-dust was placed in a safe belonging to one of the trading companies. Louis was arraigned before the local tribunal two days later, and in open court confessed his guilt and asked to be taken back to Dawson. One would have supposed that was the end of the tale. But it is not.

Among the expatriated from Dawson at Circle was an American who, having tried nearly every other avocation available in these regions, had now blossomed into a "lawyer." Doubtless he had read a few fugitive legal books in his adventurous career. He had no money, and Louis had – in the safe. There was enough for both. So he went to Louis, who was sitting in the sunshine in his open prison while the guards played euchre. He told my French cook that he was a fool to confess; that the offence was committed in British territory, and now he was on American soil, under the protection of the Stars and Stripes; that the policemen had no authority to take him forcibly back to Dawson; that, while it was easy to go down, it was hard to go back, as not more than one steamer a week passed by Circle going up to Dawson, and it took several days against the swift current; that he could prevent Louis from being taken back, and arrange matters so that the trial would have to take place in Circle; that all this caused delay and cost money, which would irritate and anger me, and perhaps force a settlement; and, finally, that for 500 dollars he would guarantee Louis immunity from punishment unless I came down there personally, which was almost impossible, for everyone knew that I was employing eighty men under my immediate supervision, besides other enterprises, and I could not spare a fortnight from my affairs on the Klondike in the middle of the short summer. All these representa-

tions had due influence on the guilty, wayward, and vacil-
lating Louis.

The Canadian officers also were decidedly out of
favour at Circle City. A proportion of the inhabitants were
enforced emigrants from Dawson, and McIntyre and Judson had been active agents in their expulsion. The ex-gaol-
birds of Circle had no love for honest law, especially for
Canadian law, but the wood-pile had great persuasive powers, and enabled them to be partially reconciled to their
exile. Yet Dawson was a cheering, comfortable place, with
drunken miners to fleece and sporting girls to love, while
Circle and the other smaller towns on the Yukon had few
of these pleasures. So the banishment, on the whole, was
very distasteful, and as a consequence the Stars and Stripes
were flung out to the Arctic sun, with execrations on the
Union Jack and those who revered its folds. One is
reminded of Madame Roland's exclamation on the scaf-
fold: "Oh, Liberty, how many crimes are committed in thy
name!"

The position of the officers in a few days became awkward, confronted as they were with a lukewarm, if not hos-
tile, judge or marshal, paying 40 dollars daily for expenses,
with no effort being made by the authorities to hold a trial,
and in daily danger of the prisoner's escape through the
sympathy or assistance of his fellow-felons, the gamblers.
Besides, Master Louis had recanted. The learned advocate
had induced him to forswear himself.

Just at this period a steamer from St. Michaels to Dawson stopped an hour at Circle. The officers boarded her,
and in ten days from the robbery Major Wood called me by
telephone to Dawson. There I was shown the written, and
heard also the verbal, report of the detectives. My affairs

were so involved that I could not possibly spare the fortnight. We were working nearly 100 men. I was my own superintendent, purchaser, timekeeper, and disburser. Besides, the gold-dust was cleared up from the sluice-boxes at the foot of the hill every third evening, and there was no one I knew well enough to trust. Even for the whole amount I could not get away. While the water runs in sufficient volume during the short summer every intelligent mine-owner utilizes all the moments as well as the hours. It was well that I possessed exuberant health, for I needed its strength.

On reflection, therefore, I could not go. After consulting with Major Wood, he sent McIntyre and Judson down to Circle with a note from me to Louis explaining that, if he would give a written order on the trading company for the dust taken from him, and deposited with them, I would not pay any longer for his "gaoling." On arrival they presented my note and an order to sign, which he did quite cheerfully – the happy wretch!

The day of the robbery, at the noon breakfast, I had gone to the cache for a bottle of wine as consolation, but it was all gone – not a single one left. Louis had epicurean tastes, and expensive ones to me. I told the policemen to say to Louis that I did not mind the bag of dust so much, but I thought he might have left me at least one bottle of champagne for consolation. The smiling rascal rubbed his hands, chuckled, and said to McIntyre: "I would have given 10 ounces to have seen the Senator's face when he found no wine in that cache."

Within an hour of his release he was paddling merrily down the river in his Peterborough canoe. McIntyre gave him 20 dollars to buy provisions, and Louis was quite jocund in his freedom. He sent me his most respectful compliments, with a suggestion that I should employ a woman cook at the chalet thereafter – an idea that I had already adopted.

The detectives, after securing the gold-dust and paying expenses, embarked on the next steamer for Dawson, two days later, quietly and secretly, for it was doubtful if they would not be themselves held up, with or without process of law. The gamblers and the jetsam of the Yukon district stranded at Circle were not enamoured of British officials, and American officials were few and unreliable, I regret to say, at that time. Subsequently the United States marshal of Circle was indicted for sundry offences to which his conduct in this affair pointed. Indeed, an effort was made by wire to detain the two policemen at Eagle, still within the American lines, to await some nefarious process of alleged law concocted after the discovery of their departure from Circle. But the steamer captain, a sensible man, gave them shelter on his vessel, and the next day McIntyre, with his companion and what was left of the gold-dust, were safely in Dawson. I recovered 4,000 dollars, 2,400 dollars having gone as toll to the Yukon River thieves and pirates. I was universally congratulated on recovering this two-thirds. One of Alex McDonald's numerous mining partners had escaped down the river with 20,000 dollars belonging to Alex, and though he had been arrested and detained for a while at Circle, he eventually obtained his freedom, and Alex did not recover a dollar. There was no one possessing real judicial power from the United States at that time on the Yukon except at St. Michaels, 1,600 miles distant, so no one had authority to try apprehended rascals from Dawson. Besides, as I have already stated, a certain feeling of antipathy against the Dawson officials lurked in all the American towns over the border. It was difficult for a Canadian to secure justice and satisfaction. McDonald could not obtain the money from his absconding associate because he was a Britisher. And it was the fact that I was an American, possessed influence, and threatened to go down myself to Circle and report the whole proceedings to Washington, that made the Circle people do what little they did to aid the detectives. On my visit to Europe a year later, I stopped at Washington and related the incident to the Adjutant-General, who promptly made the fullest inquiry and investigation. The marshal was indicted, the "lawyer" left, and to-day Judge Wickersham, an upright judge, keeps order and law paramount from Eagle to Nome, and from Skagway to Valdez.

Chapter 17

THE MURDERS

Early on Christmas morning, 1899, three men bound south left Minto, a road-house situated mid-way between Dawson and White Horse. The names of the three were Clayson, Relfe and Olson. The first two were Dawson traders going out, over the ice; Olson was the line man for that district.

They had met the night before at Minto, spent a merry Christmas Eve, and, departing early, expected to arrive at Selkirk, the next resting-place, during the afternoon.

Clayson rode a bicycle, on which he had come from Dawson and at Minto overtaken Relfe, who started on foot two days sooner. Both were well provided with funds, and the three blithely sang an old Christmas carol long after they had turned the corner of the trail leading south. The atmosphere was perfectly tranquil, and their voices came back through the crisp air and down the snowy slope as if from a mountain-top.

The blue ice-track was as clear as a Sahara pathway, and Olson traversed it twice a week watching the wire; but yet the three did not arrive at Selkirk that afternoon, nor the next, nor even the next. A week, a fortnight, passed, and then one day a telegram was received at Dawson from Skagway inquiring about George Clayson.

The trail from Dawson to White Horse is 600 miles. Travellers on it were few, and seldom divulged their homes and associations in the great world outside to the acquaintances made in these Arctic solitudes, so that the disappearance of the three might have been long uncared for, if a girl in Skagway had not sought tidings of her brother, George Clayson, who, she knew, had left Dawson three weeks before.

At once telegraphic inquiries were made, and by the next day all the North-West Mounted Police knew that Clayson and his companions had left Minto for Selkirk on Christmas morn, but had never come to the latter point. Up from Dawson the next day, drawn in a light sled with fleet-footed dogs, went Constable Pennycuick, and in sixty hours his panting team dashed up to the Minto road-side house, 400 miles away.

Pennycuick was a shrewd, energetic officer, and after an hour only at Minto he went on to Selkirk, thirty miles further, and before the day was done knew that the three men had vanished between the two places, leaving not a trace. No one had seen them since they left Minto. Selkirk, which is the site of an old Hudson Bay Company's fort, comprises a few cabins, and an operator is stationed there to repeat despatches between Skagway and Dawson.

The officer wired his tidings both north and south, and advised careful examination of all unknown travellers. The next day a man with a horse, sledge and dog, accompanied by an Indian woman, stopped at Bennett, a station some 300 miles south of Selkirk. The police barracks were near the road-house that the stranger entered.

It was an unusual occurrence for anyone to travel with a horse and a dog and an Indian woman. The whites that consorted with the Indians were too wretched and destitute to possess either dog or horse. So an officer entered the cabin directly after the man, and said abruptly:

"What is your name?"

The new-comer, who was small, slender, with black beard and clear gray eyes, was clothed in a new fur cap, new fur coat, and an old pair of shoes covered with moccasins. He looked serenely at the representative of the law, and said:

"Ross."

"Where do you come from?"

"Dawson."

"When?"

"Three weeks ago."

"Where did you get your horse?"

"Bought him at Tagish."

"Where did you get the dog?"

"At Dawson."

"Where did you get the girl?"

"At Tagish also."

"Where are you taking her?"

"Only to Skagway."

"Did you come to Tagish from Dawson with the dog?"

"Yes."

"Then, why did you buy the horse? That dog isn't sick."

"To sell him at Skagway. I hear they're high there. Besides, it's easier for the girl," Ross added with a gesture.

Now, the Indian women are accustomed to walk behind the sleds, loaded to the hips, not riding on them, as do the ladies of the south.

"Where have you been these three weeks from Dawson? It wouldn't take over a fortnight at most, with that fine dog of yours."

Ross hesitated a moment.

"Well, you see," he said very slowly, "I've been stopping with the girl's people at Tagish for a week. Why all these questions?"

"Oh, nothing. When are you going on?"

"Right away, as soon as I've had a good drink. It's cold to-day. Have something?"

"No, thanks."

The constable reflected while Ross took his liquor. It was very easy to wire to Tagish and learn if he had really stayed there a week. But the new fur coat and cap, with old shoes – there was a contradiction. And his wire from Pennycuick. He turned to Ross.

"I say, Ross, you had better come over to the barracks with me. I'd like to talk a little more with you."

The powers of the police in that locality are autocratic. Meanwhile several other constables had entered the roadhouse, for the horse, dog, and Indian woman made an odd trio.

"Very well," said Ross, "though I don't see why. What will I do with my outfit?"

"We'll take care of that," was the answer.

The horse and dog were taken into the barracks yard, the woman went over to the cabin of Skookum Jim, and Ross walked into the guard-house, whence he never went forth a free man.

A telegram to Tagish, between Selkirk and Bennett, received this response: "A man named Ross, with sled and dog, came here last week. Stayed two days. Bought new fur cap and coat at Hunker's store. Paid 400 dollars for two horses and bought Indian girl from father for 150 dollars. Said came alone from Dawson, and going to Atlin across lake. Seemed anxious get away."

This despatch induced officer Scarth to reflect again. Where was the other horse, and why did he say he was going by Atlin? The Atlin route was long and difficult, and it left Bennett miles away to the west. Scarth wired again to Selkirk and Minto, and the reply from the latter place was interesting. Pennycuick, who it seems was there, answered that two men, one small and dark, the other large and dark, had camped somewhere on the trail, but could not be found, though vigilant search had been made. The smaller man called himself O'Brien, the larger man Graves, and Scarth was advised to detain them if encountered. This description applied to O'Brien, but where was Graves? And where did a prospector or wood-cutter, "camping on the trail," get money to buy a team of horses and an Indian girl? These messages occupied some hours, during which Ross sat stolidly by the stove, saying little and seeming to be sleepy. Scarth entered the guard-house or barracks, walked straight to him, and said: "O'Brien, where is Graves?"

He sprang from the bench like a wild cat, and faced the officer with cold fiendish eyes. After a moment, however, he controlled himself.

"What do you mean?" he asked, with the same phlegm as before.

"Just what I said. Where is Graves?"

Scarth dared not say a word about the others as yet. Ross gazed into his interlocutor's face, looked at the only door – by whose open portal stood four brawny Canadians, either one of whom could strangle him – at the small window with its thick double sashes, and at the half-light of the January winter day, the birch-trees with broken branches, backing up the snow across the ice trail; then, muttering "You can all go to hell," sat down again on the cracked bench. Not another word would he say, even when a search of the sledge disclosed two rifles and a pistol with abundance of ammunition, which were brought to him for explanation. Nor even when they took off his heavy double-soled leather shoes (no one wears leather shoes in Alaska during the winter; they are too cold), and found, on removing the lower part, twelve hundred-dollar United States notes in a snug little space below.

The next day the Indian girl was found and interrogated. She freely stated that, after leaving Tagish with two horses, they attempted to cross the lake to Atlin. But they lost the trail, and getting on thin ice, it had broken under the heavy weight of the sledge and animals.

Though the water was not deep, yet one of the horses was lost, and all the effects were well drenched. There was an Indian encampment near Bennett, but the trail led by the road-house. One cannot leave the beaten trails in winter. It means to be lost and to die. So the traveller, much against his will, had made his way there, when he was apprehended. This was all she knew, but it proved to the officers that the man was lying, both as to the number of horses he had and of days spent in Tagish. Now, there must have been a motive for this, and his avoidance of Bennett was also significant, for, as it was the nearest post to the United States boundaries, the policemen stationed there were unusually vigilant and competent.

They kept him a close captive, and wired to Dawson for instructions and information, for Dawson is the headquarters of the police in the Klondike district. The prisoner was undoubtedly O'Brien. Everything went to prove that. But where were the three missing men, and where was Graves?

A man named Maguire, who was a member of the Klondike police, had resigned and gone "out" to Vancouver. He was known to possess a singular capacity for detecting crimes, a faculty which he had evidenced in more than one instance. He was telegraphed to come to the assistance of his old associates, and gladly complied. On his journey "in" he halted at Bennett, and interviewed O'Brien. But the latter was surly, sullen, and dangerous, admitting nothing and threatening violence.

He was then manacled, and Maguire went on to Minto, convinced that the solution of the mystery by which four men had gone out of the world's light lay in its vicinity. He soon ascertained that two men, calling themselves Graves and O'Brien, had camped for some time near Minto, but where no one exactly knew. They professed to be cutting wood for the river steamers during the next summer, and had no money, but came to Minto occasionally and exchanged canned food for tobacco.

These cans of roast beef and mutton, it was suspected, were abstracted from a scow that had been caught by the ice and frozen in on the Yukon not far below Minto, the previous November. But what is everyone's business is no one's business, and so no inquiries were made. Graves called at Minto the same evening that Clayson arrived from Dawson. Since then neither he nor O'Brien had been seen. Maguire very soon located the tent of the two men. The trail led across the river about three miles above, or south, of Minto, and the tent, a double one, was pitched not far from the river, and a quarter of a mile east of the road. Between the tent and the trail was a large grove of poplar or cottonwood trees, and the ground, covered with 6 feet of snow, had not a blemish on its fair surface. It was no uncommon thing for men, when going out, to leave their tent and stove, for the value of these articles would be small at Skagway, scarce equal to the trouble of transporting them, and there were plenty of road-houses in which to lodge. So this was nothing strange. Maguire knew there must, of course, be a side-path to the tent. But where did it leave the main-road? Within the tent itself there remained only a broken-down bunk for two, an empty box, a few sticks of wood, and some ashes in the stove. Very little on which to go in a matter concerning the life or death of four men. This was February, and the tragedy, if it had taken place, occurred at Christmas, six weeks previously. During this long interval more or less snow and ice had accumulated, and all traces and signs must be obliterated. He looked for a path from the tent, but the only one he could discover went towards the river away from the trail. But he felt sure that an opening from the trail at some point must have led to the tent or its vicinity, so he began to shovel the snow back for a distance of 10 feet along the road on the tent side. It is true the side-path might possibly have disappeared and left no indication. Still, he could think of nothing better; so he worked alone for five days, lodging every night at Minto.

He had two faithful canine companions who were always with him – a Great Dane and a "Husky," or Malamute. The dogs at times dug with their paws in the snow, in imitation of their master. On this fifth day the "Husky" was pawing a hole in the snow in which to lie comfortably, when he suddenly jumped back, sprang wildly on to the trail, and with a piteous, mournful cry ran swiftly towards Minto. The astonished detective called him back, but the dog would not even turn, galloping swifter and swifter out of view, still uttering his fearsome wail. Dropping on his knees at the spot from whence the Malamute had fled, Maguire threw the snow behind with his hands, sifting every particle through his fingers. A few inches deeper he found the snow was hard and icy, indicating that it had been trampled and pressed. He also observed a discoloration about a foot square in the frosted snow as he got lower. Removing this mass to the depth of a foot, he carried it to Minto, where it was melted, and the liquid sent out to Vancouver for chemical analysis. Then he waited. In a few days a report was sent him stating that the sample contained human blood. Maguire knew then that he was right, and he also realized what an invaluable detective the wolf-dog had unwittingly proved. He sent for Pennycuick, and the two began a search which, for keenness, ingenuity, and devotion to duty, has rarely been surpassed. After uncovering the side-path for a dozen feet, they could trace its probable direction toward the tent. This ascertained, they noticed that the trees in line had been shorn of some limbs, and by going to the other end of the mutilated row they had a clear and unobstructed view down the path to the main trail, and a mile up and down the latter. They discovered also that the limbs were hacked or hewed rather than cut, which they inferred must have been done with a dull axe or hatchet nicked in the middle. The rest of the tragedy is explained by Maguire's testimony at O'Brien's trial in Dawson, June, 1901, when every damning proof of guilt that the relentless champions of vengeance had discovered was produced.

"For three weeks Pennycuick and myself worked on our knees, sifting every drop of the snow through our naked fingers before we threw it aside, though the glass at times went down as low as 40° below. We couldn't take chances in losing or missing the smallest object, especially when we found a rifle shell within 6 feet of the first pool of blood. We uncovered the old trail of O'Brien and Graves up to one leading to the river behind the tent, for that is the way they always came and went. We made many discoveries, and, if your Honour will let me in my own way, I think I can tell just what happened.

"O'Brien and Graves went there for robbery and murder. After pitching the tent, they cut a swathe through branches of the trees, so as to see both up and down the trail opposite for a mile either way. In some cases they cut down whole trees also for this purpose, and made a little path, the tent being invisible from the road. They knew the three men were there, for Graves went into Minto Christmas Eve and met them. He invited Clayson and the others to take a Christmas drink with him and O'Brien in their tent, and waited for them the next day on the trail from Minto.

"When they came opposite the little side-track, Clayson entered it first on his bicycle, Relfe following; then came Olson, and Graves last. The snow path was too narrow for more than one man at a time. Just as Clayson came to a point where the path curved around some trees, O'Brien, standing in front, shot him with a rifle from behind a tree. We know it was O'Brien, because the cleft in the tree where the rifle rested is just up to O'Brien's shoulder.

Graves was much taller. Besides, a shell picked up there on the snow came from O'Brien's rifle, which was with him when he was arrested at Bennett. We know it was Clayson whom he shot first, for we traced the marks of the bicycle wheel to this spot, where the marks stopped and a pool of blood was found. Relfe started to turn off to the side, because he knew that Graves was behind. O'Brien shot him without moving from the same position. Relfe fell, but was not slain. He had a revolver, being the only one of the party who was armed; but before he could use it – or perhaps he was too weak – O'Brien ran up and shot him through the head. We found one bullet there which was flattened in the frozen muck, with fragments of bone attached. We also found a part of a tooth, with gold filling which a Dawson dentist put into Relfe's mouth just before he left, and which was shot away by O'Brien's last bullet. Near by lay an empty 40-82 cartridge shell thrown out by O'Brien from his rifle after shooting Relfe the second time.

"Meanwhile Olson had turned to run, but Graves grappled with him. Graves had only a revolver, and a desperate struggle took place for its possession. We know this, for after the new snow was cleared away the trail beneath was hard for quite a space around, showing the snow had been trampled down. O'Brien came up and shot Olson three times.

"At least, we found three of his shells there. This was the place where the wolf-scent of the 'Husky' gave us the first clue by discovering the frozen blood of Olson six weeks after the murders had occurred.

"I don't know," continued Maguire, turning to face O'Brien, "whether he shot Graves or not. We have never, though inquiries have been made all over the world, found a single trace, sign, or word, of or from Graves since that Christmas Day a year and a half ago.

"After the three men were killed, they were stripped of all clothing and dragged naked to the river, in the ice of which a hole was cut down to the running water beneath, and then thrown in. Doubtless the murderers thought that the deep current under the ice of the Yukon would carry the bodies directly to the Behring Sea, and they would be lost or eaten by fish in the great ocean beyond; but they did not know that the ice in shallow places extends near to the bottom, and heavy substances would be diverted and caught in ice projections underneath. So it happened that Olson was found at Forty Mile in May, Clayson at Circle City in June, and Relfe a week later near the Flats, 500 miles from where he was assassinated. All the bodies were brought to Dawson, and easily recognised, as also the method of their killing.

"When the bodies were thus disposed of, the assassins gathered the clothing in a pile and burnt it, burning the belts and felt shoes in the stove. We know this, for we found eyelets in the stove, and sundry little articles, such as a garter used for a German sock which Clayson wore, a black button, a safety-pin, and charred pieces of clothing. Also, crumpled up and thrown in a clump of bushes near the tent, was found a receipt given that morning by Fussell to Olson at Minto for 6 dollars for meals. O'Brien had not thought to throw this in the fire. When we had progressed thus far, the question arose: Are we sure that this was the tent of O'Brien and Graves?

"It might be contended that they had not lived there, but that it belonged to others. We sent up to Bennett for O'Brien's dog Bruce, which was captured with him. This dog was brought down to Minto, and taking him near to the junction of the two trails, Pennycuick said to him sharply, 'Bruce, go home!' The dog looked at him inquiringly, and Pennycuick repeated the command, at the same time stamping his foot: 'Bruce, go home! go home!' Bruce looked around, went up the side-trail from the main one in which we were all standing, and started on a run. When we got there he was lying down inside of the tent as if he were at home, and when we returned to Minto he came with us reluctantly. A second time dumb animals proved this man's guilt. Later we found in the ice of the river-bank a double-bitted dull axe, nicked in the centre. It fits the cuts in the trees, and we have brought down, and will exhibit in court, the section of the trunk of the tree from the ground up to the part where O'Brien cut a place with this axe to rest his rifle. It is just the height of his shoulder, and the axe has been proved to be his. He bought it at Forty Mile, and tried to get it sharpened at Dawson on his way out. Two shells – 40-82 shells that fitted his rifle – were found at the foot of this tree. O'Brien would have been tried long ago, but we hoped to find some trace of Graves. With the aid of the Government at Ottawa we have for a year searched all over the world. We know where he came from and his anteced-ents, but he has disappeared for ever since that Christmas Eve. Only O'Brien and God know," said Maguire in con-cluding his evidence.

In his cell the chained prisoner denied everything, but did not dare to take the stand and testify even when his life was the forfeit. He was promptly convicted and as promptly hanged. During the interval he tried to assassinate the clergyman who offered religious consolation, and a week before his punishment attempted to strangle the guard with his hands and escape. It was the most revolting crime committed during the several years that I was in the North-West, and the Canadian Government is entitled to warm commendation for the large sums of money expended, and the admirable tact and energy displayed by its instruments of justice.

Chapter 18

AROUND LA BARGE

In October, 1900, I left Dawson, wintered in Europe, and returned the following year. Taking the Skagway route, I reached White Horse at the end of May, 1901. After the train arrived at White Horse, I was told that there were several hundred voyagers there for the North, one third of whom were women, awaiting the opening of Lake La Barge. This lake, thirty miles long and two leagues broad, extends northward from White Horse, and is the last of the chain of lakes that constitute the principal source of the Yukon. From its northern outlet flows in good volume a clear, transparent stream of icy-cold water, forming the actual commencement of the Yukon River. From thence to its junction with the Behring Sea, a distance, with meanderings, of 1,800 miles, the river passes through no more lakes, nor are there any rapids of sufficient power and descent to arrest the course of the most feeble steamboat now upon its bosom. Though it was the end of May, and the ten o'clock sun was shining brightly at White Horse, I was told that the whole of La Barge, the southern boundary of which lies some thirty miles north of White Horse, was entirely frozen, and that it would be ten days before steamers could force their bows through the rotting ice. To stay in White Horse for those ten days was not an alluring prospect, the town being already dusty from the powdery soil covering its two or three streets, which contain only saloons, one or two eating-houses and stores, a meagre railway-station, and again more saloons. So I looked around for support and sympathy in a project that I had half formed. Meeting Judge Wood, formerly Mayor of Seattle, and his friend Mr. Arnold, both of whom I had known in Dawson, we took counsel together, and then interviewed Mr. Hawkins, the manager of the railway company, which also owns and works steamboats plying between Dawson and White Horse.

"Have you not a boat at the other end of La Barge?" asked the Judge.

"Yes," replied Hawkins, "but how are you going to get there?"

"Oh! Can't we walk around the lake?"

"I don't know, but I don't think you can. I've never known it to be done at this season in all the years that I've been in the North. It's terrible through those Arctic forests."

"We don't want to stay in this dreadful place for ten days," I ventured.

"You needn't," said Hawkins; "take the train back to Skagway, go to Seattle, and return by the same steamer. I'll wager anything you will find all these people here when you return, and the lake not opened. Even then it will be earlier than last year, for the first steamer did not leave White Horse direct for Dawson until June 15, 1900."

This was not encouraging for the impatient. "Nevertheless," said I, "what will you charge to detain the Bailey at the further end of La Barge two or three days? In that interval, if we do start, we will either arrive or send some news of our failure."

Mr. Hawkins kindly promised that, if we were determined to go, he would detain the boat by wire until something was heard from us – "dead or alive," he added
facetiously. Thereupon we resolved to make the essay.

Major Snyder, of the North-West Mounted Police,
which had a station in White Horse, promised to send a
couple of policemen in a Peterborough canoe from the station at Upper La Barge to meet and assist our party, as the
wires were up and communication easy. So at about 6:30
that same evening the three of us left White Horse in a
heavy canoe, and rowed briskly, assisted by the rapid current, the thirty miles to the southern entrance of Lake La
Barge. It was very pleasant gliding down the clear, rapid
stream in the summer twilight, and the hours passed swiftly
until the river was lost in the lake. The latter lay quiet under
its covering of ice, but at the southern and western edges
we could see a narrow margin of water. From the ingress of
the river to the western side proper was a distance of five
miles across through mud shallows. It was cold, icily cold,
a gentle breeze blowing softly over the ice-field and chill-
ing us to the core. When the boat was stopped – which
occurred often – we had to go over the side and push her
through the mud and freezing slime. Finally we came to a
foot or two of clear water, half a dozen yards wide, bordering the rocky shore, and were able to row a couple of
hours, pulling our boat over various ice blockades that
extended quite across to the land, until at last we came to
one so high, wide, and formidable that it seemed inadvis-
able to waste time in trying to get round it with our heavy
water-logged boat. We made three loads for our respective
backs, and, shouldering them, left on foot, abandoning the
vessel. Shortly thereafter we passed a canoe, stranded on

the shore and loaded with United States mails, and, rounding a wooded point, came immediately to a cabin. Without were ten hungry dogs, and within were two tired, sleeping men – the mail-carriers, who, like ourselves, had found it impossible to go either through the water or across the ice farther on the lake. During the day they expected men with horses, transporting the mails from Dawson to White Horse, to come past the cabin, and intended to borrow a couple of horses, load them with the mail-bags, and go ahead again for Dawson, deserting their broken canoe.

At half-past three in the morning, after a comforting breakfast of beans, bacon, and dry bread, we continued our journey. The sun was glistening over the white lake, and fast melting the icy films along the marshy borders on and through which we tramped. Our loads, especially the overcoats, became heavy and heavier, while the sun shone still more pleasantly. For two hours we toiled, up to our knees at times in the mud and ooze of the softening ice. Then we stopped to rest, reflect, and reconnoitre. We found that in those two heart-breaking hours, while travelling at least four miles by and through the edges, we had not made more than one mile due northwards from the cabin, which was still plainly visible behind us. This would never do, so we resolved to break away from the lake directly into the forest until we came to the telegraph-wire, and follow it northwards. It must bring us out somewhere.

A mile and a half inward we came to the line. By now it was after six o'clock, and the atmosphere was hot and hazy. We stopped.

"Judge," I observed, "I am neither cold, thirsty, nor hungry, therefore I will hang on the top of the telegraph-post this beautiful black beaver overcoat, with its manifold contents of odds and ends; also at the base will I lay these shirts and other extra raiment. If ever we get to Upper La Barge, it will have to be, not with lighter luggage, but with no luggage."

So I climbed the top and left my coat there as a black beacon. The Judge and Arnold dropped everything save what they wore, and two or three cans of corned beef and roast mutton, with some bread. It was, of course, much warmer than we had imagined or been told, and the tramp under the wire promised to be excessively trying. And it was.

The builders of the line had cut a swathe of trees 150 feet wide through the forest, felling them so that they lay piled upon the ground towards the middle, above which, on trees not felled but trimmed, ran the wire. This cut was made so wide to avoid trees falling on the line in the winter. The trees and brush in this Northern primeval forest were so dense and so numerous that it was very difficult to force one's way through on foot. It would have been quite impossible with a horse. Besides, the line was not very high, and if we left the fallen timber for 100 yards, we could not tell in what direction to go in returning to find the poles. So we had to follow the wire by the cut trees, crawling and leaping over the timber that lay thick as mosquitoes on the Yukon. The line seemed to go due north, up and down, now jumping ravines and rocky chasms, then going up precipitous sides of hills, and finally plunging down into dark glens where raged and foamed the icy waters rushing from the towering mountains to the lake. We had to follow, and did follow, through the cold streams, up to our hips in the boggy marshes, and up the steep, rocky acclivities. In one case we overlooked the lake 1,000 feet vertically below. At this point the wire jumped a slight depression in the mountain-top, and when we got there, after a most wearying climb, we found a narrow, smooth, shelving, rocky terrace at the east end of the depression, and beyond and below – the lake.

When one is very weary, one becomes callous and reckless of consequences. We never thought of going back down that steep descent again, but, without even consulting, went across in single file on our hands and knees.

After we were past, I shivered and called a rest. We lay panting in the hot sunshine, while far below and beyond, tranquil and peaceful, Lake La Barge rested, enwrapped in its snowy shroud. Ten miles opposite, on the eastern border, glistened an immense glacier with deep green and blue shadows, lying there for ever, impassable and impregnable to the brilliant, flashing rays of the Arctic June sun.

The lake was oval in shape, and one could see, from our exalted location, its whole periphery of 100 miles broken only by a few small islands, with a blue sinuous line, which looked like a monstrous serpent, cutting indefinitely through the snow down to the ice, near midway of its length. That was the road to Dawson.

We pressed on, up and down through the streams and gloomy glens, the latter heavy and rich with fernery, gilded by the sun's rays. The rotting grasses, with the fallings from the birch, cedar and spruce trees, furnished a carpet 2 feet thick and soft as silk.

Every hour we rested ten minutes, and by six o'clock we were under the 20-feet waterfall of a limpid stream, where we rested and ate the last of our food. We threw a fallen tree-trunk over the chasm, and with the aid of a balancing-pole crossed without difficulty.

Two hours later the wandering wire brought us once again to the lake shores; the level beach was covered with lava stones large and small. I wore thin shoes, and had no others. My feet were sore and I was famished. In this climate one is always hungry. But very soon we came round a slight curve, and saw directly ahead a boat pulled up on the rocks, and two men cooking over a cheerful fire. These were two prospectors bound for Dawson, who gave us beans and bacon, with pancakes made from dough kneaded with water in the open sack of flour.

We hired them to push their own boat back into the water, here a narrow channel 15 feet wide, and row us as far as possible. But after an hour's hard labour, pulling the heavily-loaded affair over rocks and ice and through shallow water, we left them and their boat and went on. The poor fellows had made the leaky, shambling nondescript at White Horse in three weeks with only a saw and a hammer. They had left White Horse ten days ago, and we had made the same point in little more than twenty-four hours.

On and on we walked by the lake border. After a few miles we overtook a couple of Peterborough canoes. The ice at this spot extended to the shore, and they were being pulled over the ice by seven men. The leader, erect and stalwart, strode 10 feet ahead of the first boat, a rope round his neck and shoulders, never looking behind, but bending sturdily to the strain when the boat loitered. We saluted him, but he did not stop. His stern purpose and determination to go on excited our emulation, and with renewed courage we turned into the forest and up an almost vertical ascent.

At midnight the sun had set, and the long twilight was gathering into semi-darkness as we stumbled and staggered on to the rocky shores of the lake, up to a welcome camp-fire. Lo! it was that of the taciturn captain with his party. But now they had stopped to rest, and received us with kindly hospitality and good cheer. We learned that it was an expedition sent out by the United States Geological Department to descend the Yukon, go up and over the Koyukuk, and come out 2,000 miles distant on the borders of the Arctic Ocean. Mr. Mendenhall, the leader, was try-ing to catch the same boat as ourselves, which he heard was below. He had left White Horse three days previously. We promised to detain the steamer if we arrived at Upper La Barge first, and remained with them resting until three of the morn. Those three hours were very miserable.

Mendenhall's party had sleeping-bags for themselves only, and no blankets. We had only our thin clothing, and were alternately frozen and roasted as we turned side after side to the fire. The air was piercing, and the little wind that came from the north over the iced lake seemed to go through clothing, flesh and bones, like an arrow. My right heel, I knew, must be badly lacerated, for it pained me intensely; but I had no other shoes and stockings, and I feared that, if I took them off, my swollen feet would not receive them again. Of course, there could be no slumber, and we were glad to start again.

Away from the lake, deep into the forest of birch and fir and cedar trees, encompassed by very dense bushes 5 feet high, went the slender telegraph-wire, glancing ahead of us in the early sunbeams like a mocking serpent. But we fol-lowed its sinuosities in silence and stubbornness. We nei-ther stopped nor talked. Sometimes one passed the other where the everlasting fallen timber, or the cold water of an Arctic brook caused delay.

The continuous climbing and vaulting over the cut trees, at times like a palisade, with the uncut limbs spreading like elk antlers, wore out our strength rapidly. But we dared not stop. To sit down and rest made it very difficult to arise and go on again. Besides, while we had every confidence that Mr. Hawkins would keep the steamer as promised, yet the fear that the message might not have been received, and the boat therefore have left for Dawson, was ever in my thoughts.

The ground altered its contours as we neared and circled the north-western margin. From mountains and deep cañons we came to hills and dales, but with more water, as the land is flatter and more marshy. Every few minutes we splashed through, not running brooks, but lakelets, and gradually, nearer the exit of the lake, all the soil that we passed over was soggy and yielding. I should fancy that at one time the lake must have extended far north of its present location, and, in fact, I rather believe that Lakes Linderman, Bennett, and La Barge, with their connecting links of short rivers, must have been originally one body of water, stretching both north and south of the space they now occupy.

The Yukon to-day begins, so to speak, thirty miles north of La Barge, for the Thirty Mile River, which gives egress to the waters of La Barge, is but a small shallow stream until it joins the Hootalinqua, from which point the river should be named the Yukon (Great River), for there it first assumes its volume and swift current.

By nine o'clock our route took us once again to the lake shore, and an hour or so later we were refreshed by the view of smoke curling over the tall trees in the crisp crystalline atmosphere. The lava rocks on the shore caressed our bruised and tortured feet somewhat roughly, but nothing could then arrest our march, and we came down the open sward to the steamer Bailey, "slow," as Captain Ballantyn said, "and a little shaky on the legs, but with shoulders thrown back and heads up like drum-majors." We had traversed, in rather more than thirty-six hours, over sixty miles of a forest that can only be compared in fatigue and difficulty, so far as I am aware, with similar regions in the smaller islands of the Philippines.

We wired our arrival to Hawkins at White Horse, who, judging from his reply, was as much astonished as pleased. Captain Ballantyne, at our suggestion, waited for Mendenhall and his party, who came in during the day. They had found more water nearer the exit of the lake at Thirty Mile, and so were able to make good progress with their boats. Two policemen had gone up the lake shore in a Peterborough to meet us, in obedience to the orders of Major Snyder. Of course, while the good fellows were pulling over the ice and poling where there was water, looking for us every moment, we were miles away in the heart of the forest patiently trailing the telegraph. They returned alone in the evening just before the steamer left for Dawson, the stanch Peterborough having been broken so badly during the voyage that they could not bring it back. It will, however, be recovered and repaired when the lake is clear of ice.

After boarding the Bailey, oddly enough, I did not go to bed nor eat as one might suppose. Extreme fatigue and hunger require gradual rather than immediate remedies. During the afternoon the boat started down the river with a swift current and clear water under her bows. I ate a couple of eggs, drank a pint of champagne and one of stout mixed together, and went to bed. At midnight I awoke, and called for the steward, who brought me a substantial meal. I slept until noon, quite twenty hours, and arose entirely myself again, except that my right heel was very sore. I had to wear a slipper for several days after we arrived in Dawson, on June 2. The Dawson papers had published the tale of our adventures as received by wire, and many were down to the wharf to greet our coming. It was ten days later – indeed, not until June 15 – that the last of those travellers whom we passed and left at Skagway and White Horse got to Dawson.

The articles we left in the forest were all found subsequently, and sent to us in Dawson, with scarcely any damage and no loss. Your packer or prospector is seldom a thief. That is for some of his more polished brethren. Although we were the first, it is said, to circle the lake at this season of the year, I suppose it is now quite common. A road may have been made since, for it is the first step that costs. In this, however, as in many other experiences or adventures, it is the initiative that is the more trying. To do is not always so hard as to resolve to do.

Chapter 19

SUMMER OF 1901

Eight months were gone since I left; but I could not observe many changes in Dawson. The usual winter blaze had not occurred, and in winter no one builds. The river would not be entirely open between St. Michaels and Dawson for some weeks, and the only persons who had come down from White Horse since the ice had gone out were ourselves, for Lake La Barge was not yet clear. So there was little alteration in numbers, and, as only few die in this healthy climate, I met many of the same genial faces, clear eyes, and stalwart forms indicating the "sourdoughs," to which I had bidden good-bye the previous October.

The day after arrival I left on the daily stage (think of it!) for the mines. There was quite a bit of snow on the hills behind Bonanza, but the creek itself was running over with water, delightful to my mind's vision, and the valley was a valley of mud and muck. Billy McLeod, who had become foreman on Dave Jones's departure for Wales last fall, met me when the stage stopped at the foot of the hill. After a hearty greeting he related in detail his duties discharged during the winter. Though he had regularly sent reports to my European address, yet no reports are so good as one's own eyes, and I was glad indeed to be back, and eager to plunge into work again. As we stood conversing just where the stage left me, we both heard a loud whirring noise, and, looking up the tramway directly in front of us, saw that the heavy car filled with gravel was speeding down the track of the steep incline.

"The cable is broke!" shouted Mac, and the words rang sharp through the clear air. The next instant the car hurled itself against the dumper at the lower end, and went through the heavy timbers as if they were of paper, dropping plump into the rushing, roaring waters of the sluices, 20 feet beneath. The empty car – for the same cable connected both – followed fast, and brought in its embrace the remains of the dumper.

"The man in the box!" cried Mac again, and we both ran fearfully forward, while miners rushed in from all sides. But Jim Ketter, the forkman in the sluice-box, was from Australia, and had lived two winters in the Klondike, either of which facts implied a capacity to take care of himself in emergencies.

Ketter could not see the accident, as the dumper covered the tramway from his vision, but he heard the noise and the shout of McLeod. Dropping his fork, he jumped from the box to a pile of washed rocks just as the car fell where he had stood, crushing as it carried boxes, gold, everything, in one mass down the steep hillside. An instant later he would have been killed as quickly and suddenly as if struck by a cannon-ball. But he clambered up on the other side, smiling if pale, and in answer to my questions said:

"Never mind, it's all right now; though if Mac had not yelled I don't know what would have happened. But this is a nice mess," he added, pointing to the ruins.

Through the mass of timber and iron the two sluice-heads of water swept, washing the gold from the riffles in the broken boxes, and scattering it down the hill. Several nuggets, in value from 20 to 50 dollars each, could be seen lying on the ground, sturdily resisting the water's impulse to carry them along. Looking at Mac, I tried to smile, and said:

"Well, Mac, it seems I've brought you bad luck! I had better have remained in Europe."

He shook his head woefully.

"I don't think," he said, "we'll lose much gold, though there was, I believe, between 300 and 400 ounces in the boxes. We have not cleaned up for forty-eight hours. Still, the gold is below there on the ground, and we'll come near panning it all up; but it's the delay."

"How many men have you on the pay-roll?" I asked.

"Eighty-seven," he replied.

"Have you a new cable?"

"No, and we can't get one in Dawson. The river is not open, as you know, and the Dawson Stores have sold out. I tried to get one last week when I saw the steel strands of our cable were breaking. We'll have to splice it ourselves. And there's that dumper and those cars – look at 'em!"

Poor Mac dropped down on the wreck, looking for unbroken timber as a father looks for his children after a Kansas cyclone. It was not a pleasant situation to face an hour after I came, yet again I was very glad to be on the spot. I left my trunk where it had been dumped from the stage, took off my nice travelling clothes, and put on good overalls and jumper.

We directed the work to continue in the mine, for otherwise the drifts might cave in, it being very wet this springtime. The pay-dirt brought out by the tunnel cars was piled on the hill terrace near my little chalet. The outside force, of about a dozen men on that shift, began at once to clear away the wreck. McLeod went up the hill to the mine, while I remained below. After clearing away the timbers and ironwork, we laid sluice-boxes on the ground, turned in a small stream of water, and with the aid of two of our most faithful men I shoveled in the gold that looked up to us from all around.

It was June, and though we worked all night there was light enough to see, even at one o'clock, when the atmosphere was most obscure. In twenty-four hours we were going on as if nothing had happened, and I do not believe we lost a dozen ounces of the gold-dust. But it required steady application, and not one of those eighty-seven men – nor myself – ever went to sleep, or lay down, until the welcome sound of the car wheels grinding on the tramway was again perceptible.

They were stanch, loyal men, and I only regret that each of them did not attain the fortune he so well deserved.

A fortnight later the force numbered 100, and in a month we were running on eleven-hour shifts, which meant twenty-two hours' steady sluicing. The two hours left were employed in repairs and cleaning up the gold-dust from the boxes. We did not waste many moments.

Water was plentiful, rain falling nearly every day. Our neighbours were quite as much engrossed as ourselves, and there was little visiting, or even going to Dawson. It was six weeks after my return before I ran down there on business that could not be longer postponed, and then I was back at the mines in thirty-six hours. But the Yukon was open from source to mouth, the whole length of its majestic 2,000 miles. Boats with hundreds of passengers were coming and going, and the town was like a beehive. The difference in active life between summer and winter was marvelous. Again I noticed a change in the costumes and the carriage of the people. Each year seemed more and more to doff the old "sourdough" ways, and bring the country nearer to the "outside." If one of the old pioneers of 1897, some of whom were yet down the river around Tanana, should return to Dawson, he might think he was not on the Klondike, but in a prosperous little town on the Pacific Coast. Nothing can arrest men's progress in physical comfort and development. Depend upon it, if the North Pole is ever attained, and gold should be found to exist there, five years thereafter one will travel to North Pole Town in good sleds with good dogs over a good trail, and find North Pole Town equipped with electric lights, tramways, and saloons. The menu of the restaurants will exhibit as the principal dishes "les viandes du Phoque et du Musc," and the inhabitants, of whom a fair proportion will be Scotch, will endure, among other afflictions, a daily paper.

There is nothing like gold or rumours of gold to lead stampeders anywhere in this wide world.

Yet Dawson did not seem so pleasant to me. The polite, smiling, well-favoured "cheechakas" were not so candid and straightforward as the earnest, hardworking "sourdoughs." There was more of the Present and less of the Past with them, and in the Klondike and surrounded by the Klondike atmosphere it seemed unreal and unwelcome. They dominated the older residents, for they had money to buy mines and other properties, and were unduly energetic, going over the whole country in a rush, but learning little.

I returned to the mines contented to stay there and work out my salvation. Oh, what an Arcadia was Bonanza Creek and its hills this last year of my vigil in the Klondike! It rained almost daily, but they were gossamer drops, and we miners revelled in the moisture pervading the ground and filling the brook with tears from the skies. Flowers swarmed over the hills, under the trees, making gardens of the roads, transforming every elevation into a perfumed terrace. As they faded and died others came, and during the entire summer and fall the country was like an overgrown perennial garden, such as I have seen surrounding the Taj Mahal at Agra. And berries, too, luscious fruit, raspberries, salmon berries, cranberries, blueberries, and gooseberries, flourished on the upper heights. It was pleasant to see the miner after his eleven hours' labour, instead of running down the hill to the mess-house for supper, run up the hill with a big empty pail, which he brought back three hours later overflowing with creamy berries. Then what a repast he made of berries, condensed milk, sugar, huge hunks of snow-white bread and coffee. The Canadian flour is the best and finest in the world. I saved money those days, for the men ate but little else so long as the berries lasted. But for two dishes their palates never palled, and these were boiled eggs and canned tomatoes. Under any circumstances the mess tables were entirely cleared of the double delicacies. There were never too many prepared by the cooks. Indeed, if some other articles were lacking for a day or so, they piled the tables with hard-boiled eggs and stewed tomatoes, and not a grumble nor complaint would be heard. Between the men and myself the most cordial feeling existed. Their wages were safe, work was permanent, and no one was dismissed without cause, and good cause. I never interfered with the foreman's privilege to employ and discharge at his will, and all Dawson could not induce me even to recommend a man to his notice. I asked

McLeod for results, and from my acquired knowledge and experience I was fully competent to know what were proper results.

When water was plentiful, the thaw good, and the ground pressing on us from the rear of the mine as we worked toward the front, a dozen men would be asked to volunteer for a few hours additional, and we always had enough. The hill thawed 100 feet above our tunnels by the never-ceasing action of the hot steam, and pressed in and down on the open spaces left as we moved outwards with our drifts.

It became not a struggle but a race between Nature and ourselves. Timbers 16 inches square have been broken in two hours after setting, and others were forced into the ground until they almost disappeared. Several cavings-in occurred, with resulting accidents, but no one was killed.

Those were happy, if hard-working, days and nights. Anxious as I was, naturally, to know if the world still existed, and what it did without me, yet for days and nights I never read paper nor book. When one is profitably, not to say pleasantly, occupied, it is odd how one can do without others, and live for the time within one's self.

The life of the territory went to and fro beneath our feet, for the Bonanza trail had become the main avenue between Dawson and the mines of all the other creeks. Therefore we were by no means lonely, even if we had time to think of such a thing, for there was never five minutes in the nightless twenty-four hours that dogs, horses, wagons, and men, were not hastening, hurrying one way or the other. However, I think I was quite as restless as anyone, for I was resolute to exhaust the mines during the season.

I went to Dawson only four times during the whole summer, and on the last evening of September watched for the last time, from the window of my little chalet, the tremendous sunset lighting up the horizon with translucent colours and silent beacons as it sank beneath the Dome.

The next day, after going to the Forks and saying goodbye to every man, woman, child, dog, and horse, in the little hamlet – for I knew them all – and also to my own faithful employes, most of whom went directly to Dawson, I walked to town in the late afternoon. I preferred to walk rather than ride, for it seemed more natural and agreeable thus to greet at my leisure wayside acquaintances, to whom I bade an earnest farewell. The pure waters of the Klondike never looked clearer as I crossed the new bridge, and the blue ice-blocks floating down the stream towards the Behring Sea seemed like departing friends.

A new road had been made from the new bridge, blasted into and around the granite curve of the mountain from the bridge to the city; new houses – not cabins, but two-storey houses – met my gaze on all sides; and the new Court-house looked like a palace, with its three storey and colonnaded Doric front. The next morning I read in one of the two daily papers London news of the day before. Telephones were in every store and almost every cabin. Wagons were watering the dusty, side-walked streets, and pears, peaches, grapes, and apricots, were for sale at street corners. Not a dollar a pear, as I had seen in August, 1898, but a dollar a box. Hay, produced in the country, could be bought reasonably, and the stores and restaurants exhibited many kinds of vegetables, grown around Dawson in quantities sufficient, I was told, to satisfy all requirements. The Yukon bank was ornamented with several good wharves, and boats were coming down from White Horse with freight and passengers so frequently that there was almost a daily mail. Food and lodgings were but very little higher than in Pacific Coast towns, and sundry theatrical notices were visible on every block. People were driving about in buggies and carriages, and an occasional top-hat could be descried, while the red shirt and jumper had vanished. The Old had been completely dispossessed by the New. I was not surprised, therefore, to find a couple of good clubs existing, and dinner-parties with appropriate costumes a daily occurrence. The few days before I left were busily occupied in settling up all my affairs and getting everything in order for my permanent departure.

On October 10 we were on the Yukon waters for the last time, and six days later sailed from Skagway. The service both of steamers and railway was much superior to the year before, and one could go to Dawson, and, in fact, make the entire round voyage from Seattle or Vancouver by way of Skagway and Dawson to St. Michaels, and thence to the same places outside, with speed and comfort.

The voyage could be made as suggested in six weeks, which would allow ample leisure for all advisable delays in Dawson and other places. Nothing is lacking on the river steamers, both food and accommodation being all that should be asked. It is a glorious June and July voyage, with undarkened nights on a river and through a country that will yet be celebrated for their charm and beauty. Alaska and the Yukon territories are amazingly auriferous.

Other Klondikes will yet be found in the vast extent of this land, and copper, with other minerals, seems to be indigenous. The valleys of the Yukon affluents, near the main stream where they are wide, will grow under the ardent Arctic sun all necessary vegetables, and also food for horses. Coal has been discovered, though not as yet of a very good quality. A man can now take his family to near Dawson, settle in one of the valleys, and sell all his produce at good figures to Dawson, Tanana, and other Yukon locations that exist and that will exist. The rigours of the winter have been lessened by modern innovations, and people who can winter in Montana and Northern Russia would almost enjoy existence on the banks of the Yukon. For there are no blizzards; I have never experienced even a slight gale. The atmosphere is always calm and clear, except when raining.

The United States Government has built a telegraph from Dawson to St. Michaels, and doubtless in time the White Pass Railway will follow the wire down the Yukon. It is the last important division of land in the world capable of sustaining population that yet remains practically untenanted, and it is well that the two Anglo-Saxon nations control its immense areas. Let us hope that, when this great country shall have been divided into states and provinces, the rulers of the Future will not, in the pride of the Present, forget the pioneers of the Past.

THE NARRATIVE PRESS

FIRST PERSON ACCOUNTS OF ADVENTURE & EXPLORATION

The Narrative Press prints only true, first-person accounts of adventures — explorations, circumnavigations, shipwrecks, jungle treks, safaris, mountain climbing, spelunking, treasure hunts, espionage, polar expeditions, and a lot more.

Some of the authors are famous (Ernest Shackleton, Kit Carson, Sir Richard Burton, Francis Chichester, Henry Stanley, T. E. Lawrence, Buffalo Bill). Some of the adventures are scientifically or historically important. Every one of these stories is fascinating.

All of our books are available as high-quality, lifetime softcover paper books. Each is also available as an electronic ebook, ready for viewing on your desktop, laptop, or handheld computer.

Visit our on-line catalog today, or call or write to us for a free copy of our printed catalogue.

THE NARRATIVE PRESS

P.O. BOX 2487, SANTA BARBARA, CALIFORNIA 93120 U.S.A.

(800) 315-9005

www.narrativepress.com

Printed in the United States
2755